Multicultural Service Learning

EDUCATING TEACHERS IN DIVERSE COMMUNITIES

—————— MARILYNNE BOYLE-BAISE ——————

TEACHERS
COLLEGE
PRESS

Teachers College, Columbia University
New York and London

Published by Teachers College Press, 1234 Amsterdam Avenue, New York, NY 10027

Library of Congress Cataloging-in-Publication Data

Boyle-Baise, Marilynne, 1950-
    Multicultural service learning: educating teachers in diverse communities / Marilynne Boyle-Baise.
        p. cm.
    Includes bibliographical references and index.
        ISBN 0-8077-4233-3 (pbk.)—ISBN 0-8077-4234-1 (cloth)
        1. Multicultural education.   2. Student service.   3. Student volunteers in social service.   4. Teachers—Training of.   I. Title.
    LC1099 .B69 2002
    370.117—dc21   2001060371

ISBN 0-8077-4233-3 (paper)
ISBN 0-8077-4234-1 (cloth)

Printed on acid-free paper
Manufactured in the United States of America

09 08 07 06 05 04 03 02   8 7 6 5 4 3 2 1

In Memory of

Lois Ruth Medley
11/7/1911 to 12/4/2000
Loving grandmother

Indy Anna
5/11/1994 to 11/8/2000
Faithful companion

Contents

Preface

I have taught multicultural education for preservice teachers for a number of years. Most preservice teachers with whom I work are white; frequently, they view diversity as problematic and hesitate to teach youth from ethnic minority groups (e.g., Zeichner, 1993). Often, they are from working- or middle-class backgrounds; those from working-class backgrounds tend to view teaching as a means for upward mobility (Ashton & Webb, 1986). These prospective teachers generally are not critical of social class inequities. Preservice teachers of color, in my classes, often come from segregated backgrounds; even if they attended desegregated schools, interracial mixing was limited. Preservice teachers from all groups need more knowledge of and direct contact with people different from themselves.

Like many multicultural educators, I attempt to bring to life abstract concepts of cultural diversity, cultural pluralism, and educational equality and equity—mostly through autobiographic memoirs, journalistic accounts, films, guest speakers, and small field studies (Gillette & Boyle-Baise, 1996). There is, however, only so much one can teach about culture, difference, and power in a university classroom alone. Community-based service learning is an experiential form of learning in which future teachers work with and learn from local communities. When community-based service learning is located in and responsive to culturally diverse and low-income communities, it can connect future teachers with constituents for multicultural education, alert them to family and community resources for teaching, and help them understand educational concerns of their future students (Sleeter, 2000).

This book evolved from my absorption in community-based service learning as part of multicultural teacher education over the last 5 years. I believed in the potential integration of these two perspectives and pedagogies. Community-based service learning offered a community touchstone for multicultural education. It provided real, responsive reasons to be in the community, and it structured experiential learning. I wanted to figure out how to *do* community-based service learning from a multicultural perspective, but also I sought ways to *think* deeply about the two fields and to study their integration. I work in a research university, where ongoing inquiry is expected. I knew my interest in this area needed to be more than casual in order to justify my attention to it. For these reasons, I began to construct a conceptual and descriptive research basis for what I now call *multicultural service learning*. This book describes my research and chronicles my journey of learning more about service learning as a companion to multicultural teacher education.

CHAPTER OVERVIEW

The chapters in this book manifest milestones on my journey toward sharing control for multicultural service learning with a diverse group of community partners. Chapter 1, "A Sense of Journey: Toward Multi-cultural Service Learning," provides a conceptual framework for this exploration. Chapter 2, "Making Distinctions: Charity, Civic Education, or Community Building," explores differences among approaches to ser-vice learning and considers the match or mismatch of different orienta-tions to multicultural service learning. Chapter 3, "Profiles: Four Views of Multicultural Service Learning," describes the perspectives of four culturally diverse preservice teachers, relates their views to a framework of meaning making, and considers three theoretical claims about multi-cultural service learning. Chapter 4, "What Really Happens? A Look Inside Multicultural Service Learning," reports findings from a field study of preservice teachers as they served and learned in community organi-zations. This chapter was written with Jim Kilbane, my research assis-tant for the field study. Chapter 5, "The Spirit of Shared Control," marks a shift in my approach to multicultural service learning and explores the nature of community partnership for this endeavor. It was written with community leaders who served as partners and coteachers during a cycle of service learning. Chapter 6, "The Exercise of Shared Control," describes and analyzes the service learning pedagogy utilized by the community partnership. Chapter 7, "Lessons Learned, Learning Lessons," is organized into two parts. The first section summarizes the research from Chapters 3 through 6 and suggests theoretical and conceptual bases for further practice. The second describes current research on multicultural service learning, delineates research issues raised from this study, and indicates directions for further inquiry. In order to capture a sense of journey, of finding a way through personal puzzlements, reflective interludes de-marcate different junctures in the book. Short reflective essays introduce Chapters 1, 3, 5, and 7.

The reader is invited to jump into this journey at points of greatest significance or personal interest. For example, theorists might be intrigued with proposals for paradigmatic orientations to service learning posed in Chapter 2. Multicultural educators might be drawn to the perspectives and service-learning activities of preservice teachers delineated in Chapters 3 and 4. Community representatives might be interested in the view, voices, and undertakings of a university-community partnership depicted in Chapters 5 and 6. Researchers might want to leap to the consideration of directions for service learning research discussed in Chapter 7. The range of people who characterized my journey and helped me learn from it should stand out from many pages, uncoupled from the linear sequence of the book. It is my privilege to share their stories.

ACKNOWLEDGMENTS

I am indebted to the preservice teachers who contributed their life stories, questions, and reflections to this book. They asked only that the information be used to improve multicultural service learning. I sincerely hope that readers find the book helpful for this purpose. I am deeply obligated to my community partners: Joni Clark, Bart Epler, William McCoy, Gwen Paulk, Nancy Slough, and Chris Truelock. They encouraged my practice, informed my research, and offered me friendship and counsel. I am grateful for years of guidance from Carl Grant, who taught me most of what I know about multicultural education. Special thanks go to Christine Sleeter, a close colleague, who allowed me to work with and learn from her. Thanks to JoAnn Campbell, director of the Office of Community Partnerships in Service Learning at Indiana University, who offered continual support. Thanks also to Karen Grady, Jim Kilbane, and Susan Johnstad for their research assistance. I am appreciative of early reviews of the book. Mary Beth Hines read numerous chapter drafts, and Jesse Goodman and Jim Langford reviewed a draft of the manuscript. A very special, heartfelt tribute to my husband, Michael Baise, and to my family—John, Midge, Brytt, Marie, and Jeff—for their faith, love, and patience throughout this project.

Chapters 3 and 4 were written with the support of a Proffitt Grant from the School of Education at Indiana University, Bloomington, Indiana. Chapter 5 was supported by a Universities as Citizens grant from Indiana Campus Compact.

The chapters in this book draw upon ideas expressed in previously published works. For the most part, articles are cited within appropriate chapters. However, I wish to acknowledge the following publications:

- Boyle-Baise, M. (1998). Community service learning for multicultural education: An exploratory study with preservice teachers. *Equity and Excellence in Education, 31*(2), 52–60.

- Boyle-Baise, M. (1999, Summer). "As good as it gets?" The impact of philosophical orientations on community-based service learning for multicultural education. *The Educational Forum, 63,* 310–320.
- Boyle-Baise, M. (2002). Saying more: Qualitative research issues for multicultural service learning. *International Journal of Qualitative Studies in Education, 15*(3), 1–15.
- Boyle-Baise, M., & Efiom, P. (2000). The construction of meaning: Learning from service learning. In C. O'Grady (Ed.), *Integrating service learning and multicultural education in colleges and universities* (pp. 209–226). Mahwah, NJ: Erlbaum.
- Boyle-Baise, M., & Kilbane, J. (2000). What really happens? A look inside service learning for multicultural teacher education. *Michigan Journal of Community Service Learning, 7,* 54–64.
- Boyle-Baise, M., & Sleeter, C. E. (2000). Community-based service learning for multicultural teacher education. *Educational Foundations, 14*(2), 33–50.
- Boyle-Baise, M., Epler, B., McCoy, W., Paulk, G., Clark, J., Slough, N., & Truelock, C. (2001, Summer). Shared control: Community voices in multicultural service learning. *Educational Forum, 65,* 344–353.

Multicultural Service Learning

EDUCATING TEACHERS IN DIVERSE COMMUNITIES

At the Juncture:
Lynne's Reflections

Often I read literature about service learning and find little attention to issues of cultural diversity or educational equality and equity. Service learners are treated as an undifferentiated group with little examination of who they are and how their racial, ethnic, and social class backgrounds impact service learning. Or, principles of mutuality and reciprocity are intoned without discussion of how differences of culture or privilege influence their fruition. Or, goals for civic education are emphasized without question of who benefits most from different definitions of citizenship.

My colleagues in multicultural education are uneasy. They worry that service learning might do more harm than good. It might be an updated version of noblesse oblige, patronage from the privileged to those in adversity. It might also exploit disenfranchised communities as learning sites for college students.

Still, a few studies support service learning as an aspect of multicultural education for preservice teachers. If utilized as an opportunity to interact with racially and ethnically diverse populations and to learn about community conditions and concerns, then service learning potentially connects future teachers with constituent bases for multicultural education. "Community" service learning, located in and responsive to culturally diverse and low-income neighborhoods, offers a community touchstone for multicultural education. It provides a reality base for multicultural concepts and for educational critique.

I stand at this juncture of multicultural education and service learning, searching for integrations that honor the integrity of both.

CHAPTER 1

A Sense of Journey: Toward Multicultural Service Learning

This book is full of people. Community-based service learning is a very peopled pursuit. Therein lies its power as an aspect of a multicultural education. Through service learning, preservice teachers are invited (and welcomed) into culturally diverse and low-income communities to work with and learn from their neighbors. The parameters of one's "neighborhood" and "community," the very definition of *us*, can broaden and deepen as educators (future and present) cultivate a sense of common concern and potential alliance with the natural constituent base for multicultural education—minority and marginalized groups, historically ill-served in public schools (Sleeter, 1996).

This book represents a journey, my journey, as I tried, erred, and proceeded toward more vibrant, critical, community-based service learning and more integral, equal relations with community partners. As I pose a sense of journey, I do not mean to imply a neat progression toward enlightened ends. Instead, my passage meandered and my aims altered as I taught and investigated service learning. This journey is based on research. Most chapters derive from study of preservice teachers' perceptions of and actions within service learning and from inquiry into a community partnership. Each investigation opened doors to another. For example, as I attempted to understand how preservice teachers made meaning of service learning, I found that many white preservice teachers held deficit perceptions of youth of color or in poverty. I invited a family, engaged in several aspects of the service learning neighborhood, to participate in reflections upon field experience. With their assistance (as well as help from classmates of color), preservice teachers' presumptions and stereotypes were challenged. This experience propelled me toward more substantive relations with community liaisons, and a partnership formed. The development and subsequent study of this partnership centered around the notion of shared control, which became a major signpost and destination for my journey.

Along the way, I gained insights from my starts, stumbles, and sojourns. I do not claim to know it all, nor do I intend this book in any way

3

as a how-to for service learning as a dimension of a multicultural education. Instead, I share my "travels" and travails so that readers might learn
with me. At the moment of this writing, four ideas are fundamental to
my thinking and central to this book: (1) A multicultural education that
includes a touchstone with disenfranchised communities is authentic,
provocative, and deeply felt; (2) community-based learning affords opportunities to make personal connections with people from groups other than
one's own; (3) service learning offers a structure for community-based
learning, collaborative in intent, responsive to local needs, reflective upon
experience, and integrated into course content; and (4) community-based
learning balances school-based practicums as part of teacher preparation
for work with culturally diverse and low-income populations.

I envision a multicultural education in which its very tenets are mod-
eled for preservice teachers. Through classroom and community-based
learning, future teachers can "live" a multicultural education. For example,
cultural diversity is affirmed and explored in reality as preservice teachers
learn from and about youths and adults different from themselves. As
another example, inequity is revealed when prospective teachers see their
lives mirrored in young parents who struggle with poverty, rather than
attend an elite university. A multicultural education takes on a face, one
no longer content with cultural celebrations of food or festivals. Instead,
multicultural education becomes a promise of advocacy for those encountered in service learning, a championship of equal, equitable, excellent,
and humane education for all learners.

These ideas and this vision for a multicultural education shaped my
commitment to shared control: an impetus to work *with*, not *for*, members
of the constituent base for multicultural education (O'Grady & Chappell,
2000). Shared control symbolizes a particular approach to service learning, one that affirms principles of multicultural education, emphasizes
community assets, empowers community partners, and potentially trans-
forms preservice teachers' assumptions. In this chapter, I explore these
ideas as a prelude to the winding road that follows.

CORNERSTONES FOR SHARED CONTROL

An orientation toward shared control evolved, in my case, from bring-
ing multicultural education, community-based learning, and service learning together and to life. In order to walk the talk of a multicultural education, it is necessary to hear, honor, and ponder perspectives and issues of
people who are disenfranchised or marginalized in our society. Community-based learning can assist this aim.

I used to think of community-based learning as field experiences, visits to and investigations of communities. For example, preservice teachers might walk a culturally diverse or low-income neighborhood and identify its businesses and services, or they might examine types of transportation available to get from the inner city to jobs or shopping in the suburbs (Boyle-Baise & Sleeter, 2000). Service learning is a field experience, but also something more. It presents real, responsive reasons to be in the community, interacting with racially and ethnically diverse groups, low-income families, or disability groups. Service learning utilizes engagement in needed, worthwhile tasks to open windows to communities. It offers a quid pro quo: Community groups profit from volunteer assistance and prospective teachers gain knowledge of local issues and concerns. However, the idea of *service* can be problematic. It often is perceived as alms for the less fortunate, rather than as an act of service in return for learning. This meaning privileges the giver and demotes the receiver. Thus the affirmation of cultural diversity, a primary goal for a multicultural education, is contradicted. On the other hand, there are juxtapositions of multicultural education, community-based learning, service learning, and teacher education that augment a multicultural education. These are the topics I discuss below.

Multicultural Education

A multicultural education is multifaceted; it is a philosophy, a methodology, a stance of critique, and an effort for empowerment. As a philosophy, multicultural education fosters regard for human dignity, respect for cultural diversity, support for cultural pluralism, and furtherance of social justice (Banks, 2001; Bennett, 1999). It is movement toward "educational quality, access, and excellence, and social equity, freedom, and justice for culturally diverse groups (Gay, 1995, p. 156). It is a set of beliefs and designs for egalitarian educational programs and practices. A multicultural education is hopeful and expectant: it expresses optimism for individual and institutional transformation; and it anticipates that all children can learn, given high-quality educational environments (Gay, 1995).

As a methodology, a multicultural education targets five dimensions of curriculum, instruction, and school policy: content integration, knowledge construction, prejudice reduction, equity pedagogy, and empowerment of school culture (Banks, 1995). For a multicultural education, cultural information is integrated into subject matter, knowledge is viewed as a social construction, democratic attitudes and values are supported, academic achievement for culturally diverse students is facilitated, and school environments are revamped to empower marginalized students.

As a stance of critique, a multicultural education grapples with dispar-ity, particularly of inequalities perpetuated against youth from cultural minority or low-income groups in schools. Systemic causes of educational failure are explored and more equal, equitable options are considered (Nieto, 1995). A multicultural education does not sidestep tough issues of racism, sexism, or other forms of prejudice, discrimination, and oppression.

As an effort for empowerment, a multicultural education is under-stood as a social movement for school change (Sleeter, 1996). The move-ment attempts to empower the natural constituent base for multicultural education: disenfranchised people in our society, parents and children of color or from low-income backgrounds, girls, youth who are disabled, gay or lesbian, and their parents. Concerned community people—parents and other adults—are viewed as potential activists, willing to pressure schools to serve their interests. Most educators are considered powerholders, members of the establishment or dominant culture. White, middle-class, female teachers find themselves in a complicated position. They often experience powerlessness within male-ordered school bureaucracies, yet still hold power in relation to students and families of color or from low-income backgrounds. As a movement for school change, a multicultural education heightens cultural regard for and provides educational resources to disempowered youth. All teachers are deemed possible allies in drives for school reform; they can serve as advocates for students and families from the constituent base.

Nieto (2000) includes all these facets in her definition of a "broadly conceptualized multicultural education" (p. 303): antiracist education, basic education, important for all students, pervasive, education for social justice, a process, and critical pedagogy. In other words, antidiscrimina-tion is at the heart of a multicultural education. It supports principles of respect for human dignity, individual equality, and social justice, which are elements of basic democratic education. It counters biased and uneven education that miseducates all students. It permeates all curriculum, in-struction, and policies. It addresses issues of power and inequality and invites teachers and students to put learning into action for social justice. It is ongoing and dynamic. It grapples with ideological struggles, contro-versies, and conflicts among more and less powerful groups in our soci-ety. Because of power differences, a multicultural education should not benefit all students similarly. While all students should acquire cultural insights and sensitivities, marginalized students also should gain greater access to educational resources and opportunities.

A multicultural education which includes a touchstone with disenfran-chised communities is authentic, provocative, and deeply felt. Service with and learning from the natural constituent base for multicultural education can shift principles of a multicultural education from abstraction to reality. It can provide clear examples of inequality or adversity which emotionally jolt preservice teachers to attentiveness (Sleeter, 1995). It can generate queries about culture, race, and power from preservice teachers, rather than from the instructor, and ground structural analysis in real, pressing dilemmas. Service learning can accredit the knowledge of local leaders and invite their views into classroom dialogue. Further, it can stimulate interest in curricular and instructional transformation which serves the needs of real youth and their families.

Nieto (2000) argues that most preservice teachers, despite distinctive cultural and linguistic backgrounds, were educated in a "monocultural" environment, school contexts which emphasized dominant, Eurocentric viewpoints, Standard English, and middle-class images. She proposes that "becoming a multicultural teacher . . . means first becoming a multicultural person" (p. 338) through a process of reeducation and self-transformation. Nieto suggests that future teachers learn more about cultural difference, confront their own racism and biases, and learn to see reality from a variety of perspectives. This process can begin, but not end, in the college classroom. Community-based experiences, such as service learning, can amplify campus instruction about a multicultural education.

Community-Based Learning

Christine Sleeter (2000) makes three telling points about pervasive views of communities: (1) Educators rarely understand communities to which they do not belong, although they believe they do; (2) educators often think they know children well, based solely on interactions in the classroom; and (3) educators commonly assume they can create multicultural curriculum by adding information they deem true about other cultures. Community-based learning can topple these presumptions. It locates preservice teachers inside communities where they learn about local conditions and concerns. It introduces children as members of families and cultural groups, with a wide range of individual interests. It helps preservice teachers realize that a multicultural education is about high-quality education for these youths, not just about attention to cultural artifacts. Community-based learning potentially assists preservice teachers in the development of key insights for a multicultural education: Cultural meanings and behavior patterns are significant to one's future students and teaching; the community is an excellent resource for learning about students; and adult members of communities can help interpret the community to teachers (Boyle-Baise & Sleeter, 2000). Each point is considered below.

Children and teachers are cultural beings. They meet in classrooms as members of cultural groups and local communities. Many difficulties in cross-cultural classrooms stem from different frames of reference for the students and the teacher. Attitudes and behavior which make sense in one context do not necessarily translate to another. For example, I work with an African Methodist Episcopal (AME) church which sponsored an "Invite Your Favorite Teacher to Church Day" in order to reverse disproportionate suspensions for church youth. According to my church partner:

> A lot of teachers who had labeled a child as a problem had a chance to see that child in a different, leadership role. It was a youth Sunday . . . the children do everything but preach. Teachers were *amazed*. When you give a child responsibilities, have expectations and let them be known in a humane way, you get positive results most times. That year, you could almost see a difference in the children's behavior in school. The teachers were more willing to communicate with the parents and with the children about issues. (G.P., field notes, 11/10/99)

Community-based learning can afford future teachers, from majority and minority groups, opportunities to compare their cultural standards and worldviews with those of groups other than their own. Direct, cross-cultural experience can help preservice teachers rethink narrow criteria for "normality" which cause cultural misunderstandings.

Academic learning is built on students' prior learning, much of which takes place outside schools. Often, prospective teachers view communities of color or low income as problematic places, which hinder school learning. In community settings, preservice teachers see youth "at home," in culturally relevant situations, where they often demonstrate skills and abilities unknown at school. For example, I work with a neighborhood community center, which emphasizes character development. Youth must adhere to principles, such as respect for others, in order to participate in and earn privileges at the center. Teachers could build upon these principles, if they knew about the center's work. According to the director, the center perceives itself as "starting where the school leaves off":

> We have a fairly good relationship established with certain teachers and the principal at the school. There are phone calls constantly going back and forth. Even though the bell rings at 3:00 that doesn't mean the child is done. Your job does not end at 3:00. The students still have a majority of their day to

learn and interact. The question you need to ask is how committed are you going to be to these kids' lives? (C.T., field
notes, 11/10/99)

Community-based learning can acquaint preservice teachers with
places like the AME church and the neighborhood center. It can help them
search for community resources or assets that underscore student learning. It can alert teachers to "funds of knowledge" (Moll, 1992) that exist
in communities, and it can motivate regard for culturally responsive pedagogy, or academic instruction connected to knowledge children bring from
home (Au & Kawakami 1991; Delgado-Gaitan, 1990; Gay, 1994; Hollins,
1996).

   **Community-based learning offers opportunities to make connections with
people from groups other than one's own.** As cultural, social, and economic
distances between teachers and students widen, it is critical that prospective teachers learn to bridge these borders (U.S. Department of Education,
1997). Community-based learning thrusts future teachers outside the
university into culturally diverse or low-income communities like those
they likely will serve. Once there, they locate community centers, meet
community leaders, interact with parents, and play with children. They
can witness vitality and cohesiveness in city neighborhoods, often centered around urban churches (Harper, 1999). They can recognize that
needs and capacities coexist in low-income areas (Woodson, 1998). They
can be a friend and be befriended. They can make connections personally, emotionally, and intellectually, that challenge false, media-informed
assumptions (LeSourd, 1997). This full-bodied experience can help build
bridges between teachers, students, and families necessary for a multicultural education (Sleeter, 2000). It can make a community not one's own
more accessible and allow one to experience culturally diverse and low-
income communities as viable and valuable.

   To the extent that community-based learning disrupts stereotypes and
constructs accurate understandings, it is valuable for prospective teachers, no matter who they are or where they will teach. For example, white
teachers who take community learning to heart can be an asset within
suburban, seemingly monocultural, schools. They can plant seeds of
multicultural understanding absent from their own educations. However,
a primary thrust of community-based learning is to target the community
as a significant source for student learning. Preservice teachers are more
likely to recognize middle-class families and neighborhoods, like those from
which most of them come, as assets for students. The challenge of community-based learning is to assist prospective teachers in developing a

resource-based perspective that extends beyond neighborhoods of privilege to those with less outward signs of capacity and strength.

Service Learning

The following description of service learning is typical.

> Service learning is a credit-bearing educational experience in which students participate in an organized service activity that meets identified community needs and reflect on the service activity in such a way as to gain further understanding of course content, a broader appreciation of the discipline, and an enhanced sense of civic responsibility. (Bringle & Hatcher, 1996, p. 222)

If this definition were written to depict service learning as a supplement to a multicultural education for preservice teachers, it might read:

> Service learning is a credit-bearing educational experience. Teacher educators and community representatives collaborate to organize service and learning activities that respond to local needs and help future teachers learn about culturally diverse or low-income communities. An "assets" model ensures a focus on community capacities and resources. Reflection on the experience includes community representatives, highlights local concerns, and considers issues of equality and equity. Preservice teachers should gain further understanding of course content, a broader grasp of the social and economic contexts for community concerns, and an enhanced sense of teaching as service to a culturally diverse public and as advocacy for educational quality, equality, and excellence.

The two definitions present different translations of the core tenets of service learning: (1) The service provider and recipient should benefit equally; (2) service and learning should be equally balanced; and (3) service and learning should enhance each other for all participants (Sigmon, 1994). From a multicultural perspective, mutual benefit upsets notions of *server* and *served*. *Program recipient* changes to *project collaborator*. An equal balance of service and learning usually requires increased emphasis on learning in communities from community educators. An enhanced service learning situation is one in which community partners, as well as students, have opportunities to serve and learn. The best example stems from a role as coteacher: A community partner serves as instructor and learns from the process. Issues of power and empowerment that are background in the first definition are foreground in the second.

Orientations to service learning range from charitable to civic, to social justice aims and ends (Boyle-Baise, 1999, Summer; Harper, 1999; Kahne & Westheimer, 1996; Morton, 1995). In Chapter 2, I grapple with distinctions between these various forms. Suffice it to say here that charitable impetuses go "against the grain" of a multicultural education. Instead of kindling connections and building bridges, charity often advantages the giver, degrades the receiver, and functions as brief, exotic visits to culturally diverse or low-income communities. Civic emphases, which aim for increased civic responsibility as a result of service learning, can augment a multicultural education. However, the language of this focus appears politically neutral—faceless, raceless, and classless (O'Grady, 2000). Moreover, there is little sensitivity to equality and empowerment in this stance (Barber, 1992). Social justice impulses focus on raising critical consciousness of inequalities and spurring responsive educational or social action (O'Grady & Chappell, 2000; Rosenberger, 2000). This stance complements a multicultural education.

Service learning can be perceived as a form of community-based learning, situated in neighborhoods, respectful of indigenous leadership, and attuned to localized assets and needs. As part of a multicultural education, community-based service learning can offer direct experiences with cultural diversity and poverty. Community-based service learning can help prospective teachers challenge their biases, wrestle with issues of poverty, situate children in their communities, approach communities as learners, and adapt learning to youth's life experiences (Mahan, Fortney, & Garcia, 1983; Sleeter, 2000; Zeichner & Melnick, 1996).

Conceivably, community-based service learning might not be multicultural in nature or intent. For example, community-based service learning could be located in and responsive to majority group milieus. Or, service learning could be situated in culturally diverse or low-income neighborhoods, but overlook concerns with difference or power. Multicultural service learning is shorthand for community-based service learning as part of a multicultural education. It refers to community-based service learning which is attuned to culture, diversity, and equality. In this book, *community-based service learning*, *community service learning*, and *multicultural service learning* are interchangeable terms.

Service learning offers a structure for community-based learning collaborative in intent, responsive to local needs, reflective upon experience, and integrated into course content. Service learning is a perspective and pedagogy; it respects experiential learning as integral to academic study.

Real, direct, collaborative experiences with the constituent base for multi-cultural education fortify, intensify, and enliven academic study. Guided reflection, a key aspect of service learning, helps jar personal perceptions and initiate self-transformation. As a constitutive dimension of a multi-cultural education, the definition, organization, and contemplation of service learning should accentuate and affirm community, cultural diversity, equality, and equity.

Teacher Education

In most teacher education programs, responsiveness to an increasingly diverse public is a central concern. Recruitment of a more diverse teaching force is one reaction. (However, it cannot be assumed that prospective teachers of color are knowledgeable about groups other than their own.) Placement of white, middle-class preservice teachers (about 90 percent of teachers-in-training) in schools with culturally diverse or low-income student populations is another option. In-service teachers often mirror preservice teachers. They predominately are white and middle-class, and commonly, they lack direct knowledge about racially and ethnically diverse communities (Tellez, Hlebowitsh, Cohen, & Norwood, 1995). School placements usually focus on the child as a learner, solely in the classroom. Some schools promote a deficit, rather than an asset, model of children and their communities. From this perspective, families and communities are perceived as faulty and problematic, instead of as resourceful and supportive. This limited, and rather negative, focus yields only a partial understanding of students and their families and communities.

Community-based learning is touted, but rarely actualized (Zeichner & Melnick, 1996). Service learning offers a means to operationalize a community-centric focus. Service learning can spur preservice teachers to think of their teaching "domain" as something that extends beyond school walls. It can alert them to work of community centers, invite them into churches, and push them to consider their students' lives outside school. As teachers, parents, and community leaders interact inside and outside schools, school-community divides can be bridged.

Community-based learning balances school-based practicums as part of teacher preparation for work with culturally diverse and low-income populations. At one point, I worked with a teacher, Mary Adam, who taught in an urban, low-income neighborhood and school for 22 years. She embodied a multicultural education. She was familiar with her students' backgrounds, advocated for their educational needs, developed instruction relevant to their concerns, and helped them understand roots of inequality. Greater emphasis on community-based service learning might help to cultivate more teachers like her.

Mary undertook about six home visits per child per year. She was well known and respected among families, and she sought their advice about school concerns. One weekend, she promised to meet her fifth graders at the local library to assist them with a research project. Few children showed up. Rather than denigrate parents or children as uncaring or forgetful, Mary investigated the situation. She called parents and asked why their children did not come to the library. She learned that safe transportation was a real problem, many parents did not have cars and had to pay a neighbor or call a taxi to take children to the library. Mary taught her students to ride the city bus, complete with transfers here and there, and she invited parents to accompany her. Later, the class analyzed bus routes, ascertained that more routes served the affluent than the impoverished part of town, and targeted racism as a cause. I remember Mary Adam because she is extraordinary; she related her teaching to the local community and helped her students grasp social relations of power that impacted it.

Community-based service learning tends to be a short, semester-long experience. A brief experience, no matter how startling or meaningful, only initiates learning—it jump-starts the process of becoming a multicultural person and teacher. This process of "becoming" deserves more than a jump start, it demands a follow-through. A series of community-based, multicultural studies should take its place alongside multiple school-based practicums as a viable avenue for teacher education. If it is important for future teachers to work with parents and communities, as Mary Adam did, then service and learning within real, diverse communities is much needed.

A VISION OF SHARED CONTROL

Shared control embodies a commitment to work *with*, not *for*, culturally diverse and low-income communities as an alliance of interests (O'Grady & Chappell, 2000). Shared control symbolizes and structures community-based service learning for a multicultural education. In this book, shared control is construed in several ways.

First, shared control underscores the need for cross-group coalitions. A coalition represents intertwined interests and egalitarian commitments. It visually legitimates cultural diversity and affirms the multicultural project. Acts of coalescence, however uneasy, model coming together across differences. Pragmatically, a coalition of diverse people, perspectives, and life experiences offers a wealth of mentorship. The proposal that "all children can learn" can be made in face-to-face terms by parents of children who frequently are ill-served in schools.

Next, shared control constitutes an educational alliance with community leaders. As classroom instructor, I can posit a resource view of the community. As community instructors, my partners can confirm and illustrate it. I can accredit community-based learning. My partners can ensure organized, worthwhile field experiences. I can propose a wealth of learning outside school. My partners can demonstrate it. I can suggest social and educational issues for youth and families. My partners can illuminate real concerns. I can support teacher advocacy for youth. My partners can share their own causes and teach their own strategies for change. Our alliance should value the community as a learning place and demonstrate multicultural education's commitment to constructive change.

In addition, shared control embodies joint ownership of the community-based service learning project. It means collaborative development of syllabi, assignments, and evaluative criteria. It identifies community partners as coteachers and coevaluators. Shared control courts collaboration, but it requires commitment and time. It bumps up against other obligations of community volunteers. To the extent possible, it is a conjoint teaching-learning endeavor.

Finally, shared control decenters the professor as the most significant instructor. It challenges the dominion of the university over teacher education. It invites community representatives into programs and inside classrooms. It proposes an unusual form of team teaching, currently unpaid and undervalued. In all aspects, shared control pushes against the norm. Yet, it builds tentative bridges to constituencies that the university claims to serve.

This book represents a journey toward shared control of community-based service learning for multicultural teacher education. I did not always fathom or practice full, collaborative, partnership for the service-learning aspect of my courses. Instead, I slowly firmed and extended relations with community partners, steadily tried out tasks that deepened community study, and tentatively chipped away at my authority for service learning. It is a tale of twists and turns.

In the next chapter, I propose three orientations for service learning and explore the distinctions among them. Then I consider the match or mismatch of these orientations with a multicultural education.

CHAPTER 2

Making Distinctions: Charity, Civic Education, or Community Building

A few years ago, I wrote an article, "As Good as It Gets?" (Boyle-Baise, 1999, Summer), that probed philosophical distinctions among approaches to service learning and considered those more or less amenable to a multicultural education. The title reflected my frustration over the impact of community-based service learning as part of a multicultural education for preservice teachers. My aims for service learning—to foster positive acquaintance between preservice teachers and people outside their immediate biographies and to raise consciousness about issues of culture and difference—largely were met (Boyle-Baise, 1998). However, my intentions to probe issues of social inequality and inequity, especially in regard to education, mostly went unrealized. Preservice teachers, especially from white, middle-class backgrounds, shifted blame for social or educational problems from problematic youth to "uncaring" parents. They judged families through lenses of personal responsibility and perceived them in deficit terms.

I wondered if the service-learning experience might not be critical enough, lacking adequate emphasis on social, structural oppression or inequity. I entertained the notion of poor pedagogy; perhaps I did not provide ample occasions to probe root causes of poverty or inequality. Actually, preservice teachers were fairly satisfied with their experience, saying that it "opened their eyes" to cultural diversity and poverty and it allowed them to "make a difference" in individual children's lives. In some ways, we were at cross-purposes. For most prospective teachers, it was enough to spur minimal individual change, through help with homework or momentary mentoring, and to become more aware and accepting of cultural diversity, particularly as different modes of learning. Often, service learning allowed preservice teachers to "feel good" about lending a "helping hand." For me, these realizations were not enough. I intended to help preservice teachers consider youth, like their future students, as members of families and cultural groups, understand the community context from which youth came, grapple with issues of inequality or inequity

15

that arose during service learning, and contemplate ways of incorporating this information in their teaching.

This mismatch of intentions caused me to wonder about distinctions among frames of reference for service learning. Educators like myself probably adopt service learning uncritically, with good intentions but with poor understanding of its various forms. I wanted to be clear about what I was doing in the name of service learning and to ensure that my actions correlated with my multicultural education perspective. I began to search for multiplicity and diversity within approaches to service learning. In "As Good as It Gets?," I posed five philosophic orientations to service learning. Then, I pondered the match or mismatch of these postures with a multicultural education.

This chapter originated as an update to that previous scholarship. As I investigated the problem further, I discovered a rich conversation about diverse forms of service by participants ranging from educators involved in service learning to religious leaders pursuing renewal in city neighborhoods. In this chapter, I engage that conversation, agree with some proposals, contest others, and push toward new interpretations. My purpose is twofold: to map variations in attitudes, aims, and actions for service learning and to correlate diverse stances with goals for multicultural education. In order to set a standard, I offer a vision of service learning that bolsters a multicultural education. Throughout the chapter, I compare various approaches for service learning to this image.

MULTICULTURAL SERVICE LEARNING

Multicultural service learning is a form of community-based learning. In order to ring true with a broadly conceptualized multicultural education (as defined in Chapter 1), multicultural service learning should be antiracist, inclusive, critical, and socially just. Multicultural service learning should center around building community and questioning inequality. It is an occasion for the "ups" to associate with the "downs" (Sleeter, 1996). The ups can hear what the downs have to say, especially about educational equality and quality for their children. For many preservice teachers, meanings for equal excellent education are abstract—learned from books. As noted in Chapter 1, preservice teachers tend to come from privileged majority groups, rather than from the constituent base for multicultural education. Even preservice teachers of color often have limited direct experience with groups other than their own, or perceive poverty from afar.

In order to build community, multicultural service learning should stimulate conversations among prospective teachers, youth, and parents. Often service as a tutor is insufficient to build community because interchange is narrowed to preservice teachers and children—parents are an aside to the process. Multicultural service learning should encourage positive cross-group relationships of trust to the extent possible in a short time frame. For example, one of my partners, an African American lay minister, sensitively advised a naive, white preservice teacher about racial issues, and, in return, the future teacher developed great confidence in her instructor (and in her own developing perspectives about race). Reconsideration of presumptions, biases, and stereotypes can stem from such relationships.

In order to question inequality, multicultural service learning should provide a framework to question the "rightness" of one's views. The consideration of "dominant and minority position perspectives" (Sleeter, 1995), or "standpoint theory" (Harding, 1991) can assist preservice teachers in understanding their views as mitigated by social position. For example, Sleeter's framework helps prospective teachers recognize that "have" and "have-not" groups perceive the nature of society differently. Harding's theory prods preservice teachers to contemplate social reality according to their standpoint or position in society. Multicultural service learning also should utilize reflection sessions to ponder inequities observed in the field (see reflective essays #2 and #3 in Chapter 6). Further, multicultural service learning should offer a space for praxis, a time to consider socially just action based upon what has been learned.

In order to build community and to critique inequality, multicultural service learning should construct equal, reciprocal, and mutually beneficial partnerships. The counsel of community people, as coteachers or field instructors, should be central to multicultural service learning. Community leaders can address issues of race or poverty in untold ways. Their voices, based on life experience, resonate with legitimacy and capture preservice teachers' attention. In my case, I traveled from scarce acquaintance with community representatives to deep coteaching relationships. The latter end of this imaginary road exemplified the potential suggested here. (In Chapters 5 and 6, community-building is demonstrated as effort to share control within a community-university partnership.)

In the next section, I explore distinctive approaches to service learning and compare each to multicultural service learning. A graphic representation of this exploration is presented first. Readers might find it helpful to refer to Figure 2.1 as a touchstone for this discussion.

MAKING DISTINCTIONS

Originally, I was galvanized by the prospect of community-based service learning as a field experience for multicultural education. I keenly

FIGURE 2.1: Distinctions Among Paradigms for Service Learning

Paradigm of Service Learning	View of Service Learning	Thick and Thin Interpretations	(Mis)Match with Multicultural Service Learning
Charity	• Provide direct assistance to needy individuals. • Meet immediate needs. • Act as "good Samaritan" or give monetary support to social services. • Enact humanism or foster altruism.	Thin practice: • Voluntary aid to the less fortunate. Thick practice: • Acts of compassion or mutual aid to worthy but needy people.	• Leaves deficit views intact. • Sometimes supports human dignity and worth. • Glosses over root causes of need.
Civic Education	• Teach citizenship education. • Promote and practice civic involvement. • Provide equal opportunities for individuals. • Work toward justice as full access to equal rights and opportunities.	Thin practice: • Compensatory activities for "at-risk" populations. • Programs are remedial. • Programs meet agency goals, have little local input. Thick practice: • Preparation for first-class citizenship. • Program planning includes local residents. • Programs flex to meet needs of local groups.	• Extends democratic ideals across cultural and social groups. • Advances justice for all in form of equal rights and opportunities. • At-risk stance allows deficit views. • Focus on individual agency disregards social, cultural ties. • Reform limited to rights and opportunities. • Liberal ends not questioned.

FIGURE 2.1: (continued)

Paradigm of Service Learning	View of Service Learning	Thick and Thin Interpretations	(Mis)Match with Multicultural Service Learning
Community Building: Communitarian View	• Communicate with others, develop mutual interests, work toward common goals. • Rethink own interests in relation to broader society. • Challenge narrow views.	Thin practice: • Communal interchange does not attend to cultural and social diversity in group make up, central issues, or tasks. Thick practice: • Communal interchange affirms cultural/social diversity in group makeup, central issues, and tasks.	• Builds community. • Practices direct democracy. • Supports mutualism. • A diverse community can sponsor a "hearing" for different views. • Seeks consensus about common good. • Singular notions of common good can mask diversity and reflect dominant views.
Community Building: Social Change View	• Empathize with others as equals. • Foster dialogue across differences. • Reduce we-they distinctions, expand definition of *us*. • Take long-term action to improve welfare of marginalized groups.	Thin practice: • Stresses empathy with others at expense of deliberation about equality and equity. Thick practice: • Makes cross-group connections. • Practices shareholding. • Grapples with inequality. • Attends to change making.	• Builds community. • Affirms cultural diversity and pluralism. • Underscores equality and equity. • Develops sense of empathy. • Fosters cross-group relationships. • Seeks root causes of problems. • Supports multiple forms of common good. • Advances change in policies, structures, and institutions.

wanted to get preservice teachers out of the university and into the community. I regarded classroom instruction for a multicultural education, even when buttressed by guest speakers, films, or novels, as necessary but insufficient. The provision of a multicultural education rests on a mindset, a way of seeing and approaching school realities from a standpoint that values cultural diversity and opposes inequality and injustice. I anxiously anticipated preservice teachers' interaction with the constituent base for multicultural education. I hoped to bring the concepts of a multicultural education to life.

At that time, I considered any placement where there was a culturally diverse clientele appropriate. I thought the principles of multicultural education, as taught in the campus classroom, would trickle down to the field, prompting greater awareness of inequality and appreciation for cultural diversity. I was wrong. I now submit that there are three major paradigms or standpoints from which to perceive and practice community-based service learning. The paradigms represent bounded worldviews. Some complement multicultural service learning more than others. Movement from one to another cannot be assumed; instead, it requires a vigorous conceptual shift. Some service learners make conceptual shifts, others do not, at least within the confines of a semester of service learning. I journeyed toward and away from these realizations by a series of twists and turns. I grapple with each paradigm through a personal lens in order to inform the byways of others.

I must note, first, that everyone does not agree that there are distinctive orientations to service learning. Instead, service learning, is thought to be a developmental process in which learners move from a personal connection with someone in need to a grasp of social problems, then to a concern for societal justice (e.g., Eyler & Giles, 1999). A continuum of engagement is posed, from a focus on charitable activities to involvement in social action. A sense of progress thus underwrites service-learning efforts. Of most interest is whether and how students move from point A to point B. What might be more curious is the character of the learner's views and the extent to which various forms of service learning disrupt or justify them. These are the concerns that drive the following explorations.

Charity

Preservice teachers generally are excited about doing service learning. Many particularly look forward to an opportunity to "help kids" and to "make a difference" in their lives through service as a tutor, mentor, or friend (Boyle-Baise & Kilbane, 2000). "Making a difference" has a range of meanings. For many white preservice teachers, it means "saving" youth through the provision of something they lack—stability, attention, or strong male role models. For some preservice teachers of color, it means "giving something back" to communities like those that nurtured them (Boyle-Baise & Efiom, 2000). I did not realize the depth of deficit views and the tenacity of missionary or savior responses early in my journey. These perceptions were revealed only through ongoing inquiry on service learning. I did not advance a missionary stance, but neither did I oppose it mightily. I categorized service learning as opportunities for "charity" or "change" (Kahne & Westheimer, 1996), but I did not reiterate this framework during reflections upon service learning. Instead, I spent considerable energy unraveling preservice teacher's deficit views and savior solutions (Boyle-Baise & Efiom, 2000; Boyle-Baise & Sleeter, 2000). My classroom teaching was, in some cases, countered by placements in agencies that took a charitable view. I did not realize at the time that a charitable placement will not make a social-change attitude. It was a case of disconnected aims and ends (Morton, 1995), a point I return to later. Regardless, I confronted an entrenched, though not intractable, stance, which I now understand as a charitable paradigm.

A number of scholars identify *charity* as a major paradigm for community service and for service learning (Chesler & Scalera, 2000; Harper, 1999; Kahne & Westheimer, 1996; Morton, 1995). A charitable position centers around giving by the well-off to the poor. There is a recognition of one's obligation to help and satisfaction in the opportunity to do so. Service learners often relish the chance to "make a difference" in the life of an individual. Kahne and Westheimer (1996) delineate moral, political, and intellectual dimensions of a charitable stance. Charity is based on a moral sense of giving, justified as a responsive civic duty, and touted as an additive experience that motivates student learning. Charity does not challenge the status quo; rather. it helps marginalized people "deal better with" their disadvantage or oppression (Chesler & Scalera, 2000, p. 19). Charitable efforts usually maintain a sense of distance between provider and recipient and exoticize people who are different.

Morton (1995) suggests that there are "thin" or "thick" interpretations of service learning paradigms. (p. 21). A thin translation lacks integrity and depth, a thick translation demonstrates both. A thick view of charity is suggested by Harper (1999) in his discussion of urban community redevelopment. Deeply felt charity is spiritually based, as unconditional love that God gives to mankind. Deeds of personal mercy or acts of mutual aid demonstrate this love. Probably, feelings of equal worth that spring from humanism exemplify a similar thick charity. In either expression, people act to meet a person's immediate needs or to support a blighted

community, selflessly, without counting the cost. A thin approach to charity is estranged from its spiritual or humanistic base. Individuals give lightly
of their time and energy as a handout to the less fortunate.

I have witnessed the power of spiritual beliefs to motivate deep examination of biases and stereotypes, particularly for white prospective
teachers (Boyle-Baise & Efiom, 2000). A deeply felt sense of charity does
not counteract multicultural service learning. Caring profoundly for another human being denies denigration and sponsors respectful assistance.
Unconditional love offers an opening to assist preservice teachers in making a conceptual shift away from charity toward community-building orientations to service learning.

Weak or thin forms of charity provide temporary assistance, but do
not question underlying bases for social ills. If perceived as a form of bene-
faction, it can be little more than noblesse oblige (O'Grady & Chappelle,
2000, p. 209). Thin charity does nothing to cultivate a broader sense of
community or to question inequality. Arguably, it hampers community
by allowing a shallow form of social support. It is this sense of giving that
is most uncomfortable for multicultural service learning.

I still fret about disjunctions between charitable views and principles
for a multicultural education. I continue to grapple with ways to move
preservice teachers beyond charitable views. Yet, I am intrigued by Morton's
(1995) resolution to this problem. He proposes that instructors worry less
about conceptual shifts and offer more support for students to enter more
thickly or deeply into their current paradigm. He encourages educators to
recognize integrity in deep approaches to several forms of service learning. From a multicultural perspective, this translates to respect for spiritual and humanistic perceptions of service as charity.

Harper (1999) describes "social service" as another paradigm. Unem-
ployment compensation, aid to dependent children, and food stamps are
forms of social service. Harper describes social service as a mass version of
charity: Programs meet immediate needs in an efficient, coordinated, accountable manner. Social service agencies typically operate as bureaucratic
systems, distanced from the people served. Nevertheless, they provide a
charitable outlet suited to busy citizens who give their money, but not their
time. Social service seems to me to be another charitable venue, rather
than a separate paradigm. To the extent that social service creates depen-
dency, it is a thin form of charity. Some social service programs, especially
for youth recreation, offer positive outlets for youth participation. They
represent thick charity and often slide into the civic education paradigm,
described below.

I have found placement in some social service agencies troublesome
for multicultural service learning. Programs for youth are plagued by a

compensatory, deficit mentality. Preservice teachers soak up a deficit stance and describe youth with labels: "that learning disabled child," or "that child from a terrible home." Community centers operate compensatory programs too, but there is a sense of doing something positive, of building character, for example, rather than acting as a caretaker. Some social service agencies, like Head Start, are mandated to include parents in key decision-making roles. Such agencies defy easy characterization. Usually, compensatory impulses mingle with respect for local families. I find experience in a place like Head Start a mixed bag for multicultural service learning.

Civic Education

I have a favorite tee shirt, given to me by the director of a community center where I work. It reads: "Character counts! Kids can make a difference in the world." A racially mixed group of cartoon kids hold signs reading: "Caring," "Fairness," "Respect," "Responsibility," "Citizenship," and "Trustworthiness." On the back, the shirt says: "Caution, Role Model at work!" The shirt's motif is clever and fun, but it also concerns me. I wonder why character traits of criticism or activism are not included. I worry about the kind of role I should model. In order to foster equality and equity, youth should learn to critique their life circumstances and to work collectively to improve them. As a role model, I should assist their social examination and support their efforts for change. From a multicultural perspective, the shirt's message should be recast to: "Equality Matters!" or "Appreciate Diversity!" The children might carry signs announcing: "Have Courage," "Be Counted," "Ask Questions," "Take Action," and "Fight for First-Class Citizenship." Still, I wear the tee shirt, proud to advertise the work of the center. Its programs benefit from local input, focus positively on youth's capacities, and foster individual growth. They exemplify and are situated within the civic education paradigm.

The civic education paradigm is ubiquitous to service learning (Battsioni, 2000; Ehrlich, 1997; Eyler & Giles, 1999; Gabelnick, 1997; Vadeboncoeur, Rahm, Aguilera, & LeCompte, 1996; Wade & Yarbrough, 1997). Within a civic education stance, citizenship is developed through service. Four themes resonate through literature on civic education: collaboration with community, importance of reflection, active learning, and development of empathy. The knowledge and skills that service learning enhances supposedly strengthen social awareness, promote civic responsibility, and foster action to meliorate social problems.

Much of the language surrounding this orientation seems politically neutral. However, Varlotta (1997) argues that Rawls' liberal contract theory

(1971) underpins this stance. According to Rawls, rational people, who think of themselves as randomly born, without knowledge of their race, ethnicity, gender, or social class, will act fairly to secure rights and opportunities for the least socially advantaged. Justice depends upon equal access to scarce resources and equal chances to utilize them. Availability and opportunity are standards of fairness. Individuals who are, supposedly, autonomous should profit from equal opportunities and advance themselves. Action on behalf of the least advantaged serves one's enlightened self-interest. For example, service as a tutor helps youth take advantage of their education and, simultaneously, helps develop educated, productive, future fellow citizens.

Character Counts! is a program that embodies these views. "Virtues" of self-reliance are fostered, amidst a climate of fairness to everyone. Good citizenship centers around "good" "character." Hypothetically, caring, responsible, trustworthy individuals will create a better world.

Varlotta (1997) submits that, in service-learning discourse, a liberal view often is entangled with a communitarian stance. Civic responsibility is defined as collective action toward the common good. Benjamin Barber (1992; 1998) is a notable proponent of this blended position. According to Barber, service learning assists the reinvigoration of citizenship. It aids student-citizens in understanding that their rights depend upon their responsibility to be civically active. Service learning develops dispositions and skills for collaborative, deliberative civic participation. Barber champions a "strong democracy focusing on mutualism, active pursuit of common goods, and creative common action" (1998, p. 74). He holds that "thin," representative democracy encourages passivity and whittles citizenship down to voting.

Morton (1995) proposes "project" as another paradigm for service learning, yet this stance resonates with civic education. According to Morton, community organizations address community needs primarily through projects. Organizational leaders "get something done," for example, to help children achieve in school or to make youth more employable. Directors of community organizations strive to create opportunities for their clientele with scarce resources. There is little sense that social institutions might be fundamentally flawed. Instead, people's lack of ability or opportunity to participate fully in society is perceived as a major concern.

Projects that promote equal access to scarce resources, like English-language instruction for immigrant families or after-school tutoring for low-income youth clearly invoke liberal contract theory. Service learners act to "equal the playing field" and thus benefit the least advantaged. Projects often demonstrate communitarian conviction as well. When preservice teachers observe parent or board meetings in which projects are planned and monitored, they see strong democracy at work. Citizens develop ways to extend opportunities to more individuals in the neighborhood.

Projects usually operate as Band-Aids, or temporary redress for social problems. For example, character counts, but good character does not necessarily open job possibilities or afford college educations for those in poverty. Additionally, program guidelines often are preset elsewhere, at the city level for the community center or at the federal level, in the case of my work with Head Start. Community folks operate inside a box defined by liberal goals for equal access and opportunities. Two problems develop for multicultural service learning: (1) A focus on individual opportunities disregards social forces for inequality; and (2) collaborative action does not actually well-up from community residents and represent their ideas. As part of multicultural service learning, a program-by-program solution to social ills should be critiqued.

My own aim to involve directors of community programs as coteachers, to share control, works against project critique. Directors usually discuss their programs in a language of opportunity and collective goodwill that seems beyond doubt. Most preservice teachers find it hard to question respected goals for equal opportunities, to ask "equal opportunities for what?" Further, it is difficult to interrogate neighborhood involvement and show it to be less self-determined than it seems.

Community-Building

A third service learning paradigm joins two unlikely bedfellows: communitarian and critical or social justice views. I imagine the two perspectives as divergent discourses enveloped within a single paradigm. An impetus to build community characterizes both. For communitarians, community-building focuses on processes of civic deliberation and action: stating, hearing, and weighing concerns, considering resolutions on behalf of the common good, then acting toward that good. In the social justice view, it is this process and more. For social change adherents, issues of inclusion, antiracism, equality, and justice should characterize and direct deliberations. Explicit attention to culture, race, difference, and power is expected. In aims to foster connectedness, collaboration, and civic betterment, the two camps overlap. In pursuit of the common good and in critique of the status quo, the two stances vary. I sketch each view separately and suggest possible interchange between them.

A Communitarian View. I was invited to speak publicly about community-building as an aspect of service learning. I described my partnerships with community associations, highlighting the need to develop pluralistic coalitions and to attend to issues of culture and difference. Surprised, my host had expected me to talk about the feeling of community, the atmosphere of goodwill, sincere study, and frank conversation, that she sensed during her visits to my class. Each of us had in mind a different interpretation of community-building.

The cultivation of community as a place of mutual regard, common interest, openness, and acceptance is fundamental to multicultural service learning. It allows sincere and serious conversation about issues of culture, race, and equality to develop. It prompts preservice teachers and community partners to share personal experiences and to learn from them. I painstakingly nurture solidarity and fellowship, an esprit d'corps if you will, among the parties with whom I work. For preservice teachers, I organize plenty of work in cooperative, mixed-race groups, toward common goals. For community partners, I continually demonstrate my sincerity as a teacher and a learner, especially as a person who can learn from them, and I share my power as university instructor, a point discussed fully in Chapter 5. These efforts lay the groundwork for community-building, of either a communitarian or social change bent.

For communitarians, what gets done among a cooperative group is significant. Community-building involves the coming together of individuals to join forces, develop mutual aims, and take common actions. Theories of John Dewey often undergird this position. Dewey (1916/1966) perceived democracy as an ideal of associated living, grounded in the participation of individuals in public life. Democratic participation requires a "scientific morale" or a willingness to deliberate ideas and, possibly, to change one's position in the process (Dewey, cited in Festenstein, 1997, p.87). Dewey recognized that what he called virtues of tolerance, open-mindedness, and imaginative sympathy foster a willingness to entertain other's positions. According to Dewey, deliberation can be transformative: it can exercise intelligence and contest narrow views. Ideally, individuals can mesh their interests with those of their larger community, and interests of separate groups can harmonize with one another. The following selections exemplify a communitarian approach in my classroom and with my community partners.

Preservice teachers in my multicultural education course are organized as service-learning teams. Teams are mixed by race, class, gender, and home region. The teams serve in the community together; they share rides, attend the same events, and identify as a unit. Service-learning teams complete a joint inquiry project. Their inquiry stems from a site-generated question of mutual interest. They act as a cooperative group during reflective discussions, meeting in small groups to raise points for large group interchange. The teams communicate intensively, deliberate collectively, develop mutual interests, and work toward common purposes.

I think of my community liaisons as partnerships, a term that signifies mutualism, reciprocity, and equality. I designate my efforts as "sharing control" and facilitating a "community of teachers." The partnership meets regularly over the summer to collectively develop the syllabus, assignments, and evaluation formats for multicultural service learning. We work as peers to construct a service-learning experience that affirms cultural diversity, confronts adversity, and recognizes assets in low-income communities. Through our tasks, we develop a sense of solidarity and common purpose.

Community-building as fellowship or as joint endeavor needs to stretch to accommodate tenets of a multicultural education. Those who come together should be culturally diverse, including people often at the margins of public deliberation and action. Purposes and aims should expressly address issues of equality and equity. Diversity should be honored, even if it creates contention. Actually, readiness to disagree and to offer multiple viewpoints should be thought of as an aspect of goodwill.

For multicultural service learning, "thick" communitarian impulses acknowledge difference and expect divergence. Disagreement, conflict, and multiplicity are valued results of conjoint endeavors. Service-learning initiatives that respond to this view ensure diverse representation, sponsor inclusiveness, confront discrimination, and seek a common good that is just and fair.

A Social Change View. A number of scholars propose a paradigm of social critique and change (Chesler, 1995; Chesler & Scalera, 2000; Harper, 1999; Kahne & Westheimer 1996; Morton, 1995; Rhoads, 1997; Rosenberger, 2000; Varlotta, 1997). This stance is identified with multiple terms such as *systemic justice, social change, critical community service*, a *Freirean perspective*, or a *discourse practice community*.

From a social change position, Dewey's proposals (and the communitarian position) fall short. Commonly, there is little express attention to culture, race, and power. It is presumed that people find it in their mutual interest to stop injustice. For example, theoretically a group of intellectually engaged people will challenge narrow and exclusive views. From a social change perspective, it is unlikely that racism and other forms of discrimination will be challenged unless those who are excluded begin to be heard. Further, unless concerns with inequality are unequivocally targeted, conjoint endeavors are unlikely to challenge the status quo.

Social change adherents believe it is important to search for root causes of injustice and to build a sense of collective power. They view oppressed people as having assets and skills to act on their own behalf. Sleeter (2000) and Woodson (1998) describe this outlook as a "resource" or "capacity-driven" view. The social change position takes a long view of social betterment, rather than a program-by-program approach to immediate problems. Partnership between local communities and outside resource groups is emphasized, but paternalistic relations are avoided.

Like their communitarian counterparts, advocates for social change submit that a "spirit of true connectedness" stimulates and sustains community (LeSourd, 1997, p. 158; see also Radest, 1993; Rhoads, 1997; Rosenberger, 2000). Supposedly, emotional connectedness is based on empathy with people unlike oneself. Rhoads positions an ethic of care at "center stage" for "critical service learning" (p. 90). However, empathy and a sense of community sometimes are pushed to the side. Social, systemic critique takes center stage. It is the spirit of connectedness that joins these two camps. Like Rhoads, I submit that this spirit underpins efforts for social change and should not be diminished.

Chesler (1995) points out three confusing aspects of service learning for social change. First, the promotion of individual learning does not necessarily lead to social change. Learning focused on individual change—for example, the disruption of stereotypes—develops a tolerant mind-set, but does not constitute social change. Second, service learners who fit into prescribed roles in social service organizations do not usually question the nature or quality of their activities. Third, in order to imagine how service learning can be change making, clear goals for change and a realistic notion of social change making are needed.

Occasions for authentic advocacy or institutional change are rare for multicultural service learning. More likely, service learning offers opportunities to prepare future teachers to be change makers in schools. For example, prospective teachers who witness assets of low-income communities are less likely to denigrate them and more likely to utilize local resources as part of their future teaching. As another example, future teachers who understand how to conduct field studies inclusive of in-group or local perspectives possess a tool for learning about their students and for connecting school studies to home lives.

Still, it is important to search for opportunities for preservice teachers to engage in social or institutional change. In my case, preservice teachers' participation in the establishment of a tutoring initiative at the African Methodist Episcopal (AME) church exemplified social change. This effort did not stand out so much for its substance—youth were tutored primarily on school assignments, as is usually the case—but, the tenor of the effort illustrated aspects of social change.

Preservice teachers worked with their community instructor and the church pastor to develop and operate the tutoring program. It was introduced, then later lauded, during church services. Parents requested tutoring services and, sometimes, provided directions for it. Parents or other church members were present during tutoring sessions, and they encouraged academic achievement. They pointed to preservice teachers as collegiate success stories, a goal for their own children.

In order to heighten potential for social change, this initiative could be modified so that preservice teachers offer mentorship beyond common homework tasks. Possibly, preservice teachers could provide college-prep workshops or discussions. For this round of service learning, I was pleased with preservice teachers' grassroots, ground-floor involvement in the creation and implementation of a self-help project.

Multicultural service learning is not belittled by a focus on individual change. A central purpose of the experience is to make personal connections with people different from oneself, to participate, albeit momentarily, in their lives, to hear their views and, in response, to reconsider one's own. Service learning can emotionally jolt preservice teachers to learn more about cultural diversity and pluralism, to examine their own biases and racism, and to learn to see reality from a variety of perspectives (Sleeter, 1995). As noted in Chapter 1, a process of reeducation and self-transformation is key to becoming a multicultural person and teacher (Nieto, 2000) and serves future teachers no matter who they are or where they work.

"Working with" community partners as coteachers is pivotal to a community-building, social change stance. Issues related to culture, racism, and poverty often arise during service learning. As instructor, I respond generally to issues, but I often misunderstand local exigencies. My partners offer alternative outlooks, locally attuned. Their input diversifies what preservice teachers can learn. Moreover, they grapple with equality and equity as issues arise in the field. For example, one community partner reported the following conversation, between herself and a preservice teacher, relating to an incident during a tutoring session at the AME church.

> One of our students was white. Our young boys played with her hair. They made observations that her hair was so silky and that her lips were so pink. It gave me a chance to talk about some of the issues we deal with as a black race, about black men and white women. I learned how naive these young people are and how TV and media influence their thinking about culture. It gave me a chance to speak to what they were talking about. (G.P., interview, 12/10/99)

As another example, a community partner shared his surprise over racial attitudes expressed in reflective essays. This passage also indicates an opening to discuss change making with a particular preservice teacher.

> Yes, I saw racial stereotypes, but my group was different.
> One of my students admitted that he did not realize how
> racially stereotypical he was until then. I don't think these
> reflective essays should ever be dismissed from this portion
> of the curriculum. It really lets us know where they are, what
> they learned. I was just amazed at what we take for granted.
> Even myself, being raised in a large city, I took for granted
> that people were people. Race wasn't in a spotlight as much
> as it is here. One student asked me, how can I become a
> more multicultural educator. That is the whole point of this
> project! (W.M., interview, 12/10/99)

I have found that predominately black churches (i.e., churches with African American leadership and style, predominately black or mixed in congregation) often bring a social change perspective to life. African American identity is affirmed and celebrated. Social equality is addressed in sermons and in church conversations. Self-help programs, from life lessons for teens to development of resumes, support taking personal responsibility for one's life. The churches demonstrate an asset and advocacy stance toward their congregants. Many white preservice teachers experience this affirmative posture for the first time. Some preservice teachers of color select the churches as spaces of respite from a predominately white university context. They feel that, through church work, they "give something back" to people from their own racial group (Boyle-Baise & Efiom, 2000).

Literature about the role of local leaders and churches, particularly Catholic and African American churches, in the restoration of urban communities has informed and underscored my continuation of church partnerships. Urban neighborhood churches often are part of the "natural immune systems of urban communities" (Woodson, 1998, p. 34). They are centers for self-development and neighborhood renewal: they offer programs for self-growth, build low-income housing, organize health centers, construct schools, and provide jobs (Flake, 1999; Harper, 1999). Multicultural service learning can benefit from links to community-building efforts such as these. Future teachers can learn of a local resource and also experience a "thick" sense of change making. In urban and African American churches people often work together, without preset rules, to take charge of their own lives.

(MIS)MATCH WITH MULTICULTURAL SERVICE LEARNING

As already stated, my vision for multicultural service learning centers around building community and questioning inequality. It should kindle connections between preservice teachers and youth, parents, and other adults in culturally diverse or low-income communities. It should help preservice teachers understand their future students outside the classroom, as they are perceived in their own homes and neighborhoods. It should spur prospective teachers to rethink their prior views of race, culture, equality, and equity. And it should offer occasions to partner across lines of race, culture, and social class. To what extent do the three paradigms—charity, civic education, and community-building—match or mismatch aims for multicultural service learning?

Charitable dispositions largely are problematic for multicultural service learning. Charity advantages the giver, humbles the receiver, avoids core causes for inequality, and skirts questions of fundamental reform. Charity stimulates a false sense of restitution—givers "feel good" about making a momentary difference. However, thick charity, as spiritual love or humanistic respect, can motivate unselfish efforts to relieve destitution, restore human dignity, and build a more humane world. This form of charity is compatible with multicultural service learning.

The liberal stance that underpins civic education can assist aims of multicultural service learning. Democratic ideals espouse first-class citizenship for all. Individuals are considered equal in terms of rights and opportunities. Efforts to secure freedom for all through civic activism is endorsed. An extension of democratic rights and opportunities across cultural and social groups augments multicultural education. However, it is impossible to regard individuals as unencumbered, apart from their group memberships. The status of one's group often impacts one's exercise of rights or access to opportunities.

Tutoring programs usually are a thin form of civic education. College students (such as preservice teachers) offer help with homework, but the type of homework low-income youth receive (often remedial, skills and drills) or how doing homework fits into their current or future lives is unquestioned. The tutoring program at the AME church, alternatively, espoused academic achievement as part of the road to a collegiate future. Unfortunately, the focus of tutoring—homework assignments—was quite usual. Had we altered tasks to genuinely assist youth in taking full advantage of their schooling, this initiative might illustrate thick civic education. Had we worked with parents and church members to advocate for youth in the project, it might demonstrate social change more strongly.

Community-building can be a powerful force for multicultural service learning. It is important to engender a sense of solidarity and to construct collectives, among preservice teachers and in the community. Communitarian sensitivity to mutual regard, open exchange, careful deliberation, and common interest can underpin and guide the development of community. Ideally, if groups are culturally diverse, honest dialogue that crosses borders of race, ethnicity, and poverty can begin. Participants can hear where others are coming from, perhaps for the first time. Frank conversation about realities, dreams, and concerns can spark ties that bind. We-they barriers can decline.

The communitarian stance is constrained by lack of direct attention to diversity and pluralism. In fairness, Dewey (1916/1966) worried that social class stratification posed a barrier to the free interplay of ideas. He envisioned an unrestricted forum in which robust argument challenged insular views. In order to achieve this forum, exclusivity in all its forms needs to be prohibited. Instead, affirmation of diversity needs to be part of the fabric of community-building, from group composition to the topics discussed, to the actions pursued. Communitarian emphases on commonality can mute difference. This position needs to be reconsidered. In a communal, but culturally diverse context, multiple dispositions should be heard and plural common goods should surface. For multicultural service learning, it is necessary but insufficient to develop a space for honest dialogue and thoughtful deliberation. The nature of the conversation, who participates in it, and what happens as a result of it matters.

A social change view of community-building complements multicultural service learning. Culture, difference, and power should be addressed in the selection of community partners, the nature of field tasks, the substance of reflective activities, and the criteria for evaluation. University and community liaisons should demonstrate linkages across social and cultural groups. Empathy with life struggles of people different from oneself should be valued. Issues of power, powerlessness, and empowerment should be unpacked. Recognition of multiple understandings of social good should be underscored. Community assets should be sought and exemplified. Equal partnerships should set the standard for university-community relations.

Chesler's (1995) caveats are significant here. In my experience, a social change orientation impacts preservice teachers' learning mostly as attitudinal and behavioral change. It is unlikely that preservice teachers will act to bring about genuine social change in the context of service learning. Instead, multicultural service learning can be utilized to shape dispositions and to build skills for later change making in schools. A thick practice of social change, whether focused on individual change or on preparation for change making, should affirm cultural diversity and address racism, classism, and other forms of bias and inequity.

Why did I struggle with service learning that was not critical enough? The problem was both conceptual and practical. I did not fully grasp distinctions among various paradigms for service learning, and I foiled good intentions with poor pedagogy. Morton (1995) speaks to one troublesome aspect of my approach: disconnected aims and ends. Morton's college students tutored youth and cared for infants at an AIDS center. They gained understanding about individual needs, but they did not correlate their experiences with his teaching about racism. Morton's teaching aims were disconnected from the ends of service learning.

When an instructor's goals mismatch the nature of the service-learning experience, then frustration, for the instructor and for the students, often follows. A charitable task probably will not generate insights for social change. Similarly, experience within a self-help group probably casts charity aside. Morton (1995) submits that "the irony of service-learning in higher education is that we assume that the learning consequences of service may differ significantly from the nature and immediate purpose of the service itself" (p. 29). A mismatch between course goals and field experiences mitigates those aims. In my case, I sometimes placed preservice teachers in social agencies with compensatory views. Then I expected these teachers to disavow deficit outlooks and wondered why they did not.

Additionally, I did not sense the paradigmatic force of bounded worldviews. A shift from a charitable to a liberal stance requires the casting aside of deficit perceptions. A shift from a liberal to a social change position demands rethinking meritorious views. I needed to wrestle with the impact of deeply held, paradigmatic positions on teaching and learning.

Instructors and prospective teachers potentially approach service learning from distinct and dissonant paradigms. While I fretted about service learning that was not critical enough, many preservice teachers probably found their experiences quite critical, daring, and novel. The challenge is to recognize the paradigm within which one works, or aims to work, and within which preservice teachers make meaning of service learning. It is a tall order. A good beginning lies in thinking deeply about our orientation to service learning, then finding ways to do what we mean. We reap what we sow.

In this chapter, paradigms for service learning were distinguished. A community-building paradigm was introduced. Thin and thick interpretations of each orientation were suggested. Parameters for multicultural service learning were indicated. The correlation of different paradigms to multicultural service learning was discussed. This exercise was intended to clarify and recommend choices for service learning that enhance a multicultural education.

In the next chapter, diverse individual service learners are profiled. The ways in which these service learners, preservice teachers in a multicultural education course, interpret service learning is described. The community-building paradigm framed their experience and impacted their perceptions of service learning.

A Research Base:
Lynne's Reflections

When community service learning is linked to multicultural education, there is very little evidence of what happens and what preservice teachers think about it. I seek to move the discussion of this linkage beyond prescriptions and anecdotes. In the research that follows, I attempt to build a descriptive foundation for inquiry into multicultural service learning.

I do not consider my investigations exemplary, but rather examples of research on community service learning pursued from a multicultural perspective. For example, when I developed personal profiles of prospective teachers as service learners, I selected men and women from diverse backgrounds, then pondered the impact of biography upon their views. Or, when I studied what happened in the field during service learning, I pondered the connections between my ideals for multicultural education and experiential realities.

At the risk of losing readers who find investigative detail boring, I lay ground work for scholars and practitioners who follow. My journey is one of learning more about community service learning and how it might robustly underscore multicultural education. It is a journey grounded in research and driven by reflection upon my inquiries.

CHAPTER **3**

Profiles: Four Views of Multicultural Service Learning

Doing community service and working with white kids and kids of color, I learned a lot. Even though they were little, they taught me something. Now, I realize that white kids have struggles in school too, like kids of color. I learned that black and white kids both think the other group does not like them. As a teacher, I would play that game with brown eyes and blue eyes [a simulation for elementary children that deals with discrimination]. Kids need to know how it feels to be treated badly by another racial group. (C.R., interview, 12/4/98)

Early on my journey, my research focused on the identification of general categories of meaning among prospective teachers who participated in multicultural service learning. I started by studying my own courses. Then I combined my data with that of a colleague doing similar work. Based on this larger sample, a framework of preservice teachers' perceptions of multicultural service learning was developed. Always I searched for the general case. In this chapter, I do the opposite. I focus on a small, diverse group of preservice teachers in order to tease out their idiosyncratic views. First, I summarize my earlier research and situate it within the three paradigms described in Chapter 2. Second, I present profiles of four preservice teachers from varied racial or ethnic groups and social class backgrounds. Third, I analyze the profiles for shared meanings, conceptual categories, and paradigmatic views. Last, I consider ways in which these profiles inform the practice of multicultural service learning.

PRIOR STUDIES

My first investigation of multicultural service learning was a case study of the perceptions of 65 European American, middle-class, prospective teachers (Boyle-Baise, 1998). Subsequently, Christine Sleeter and I searched for patterns of meaning among preservice teachers who had participated in multicultural service learning over a 4-year period, in the Midwest and on the West Coast (Boyle-Baise & Sleeter, 2000). I rolled data from my first study into this larger case. A sample of 104 European American preservice teachers and 13 African, Mexican, and Asian American preservice teachers was created. Regardless of regional, course, and service-learning differences, a framework of meaning emerged. Inasmuch as the second study built upon the first, only the findings from the second study are reported here.

Based on preservice teachers' reflective essays, final papers, and interviews, Sleeter and I identified four perceptions of multicultural service learning: deficit, affirmative, pragmatic, and activist views. Preservice teachers did not necessarily progress from one extreme to the other, as on a continuum from deficit to activist views. Instead, most future teachers came to service learning with particular views, then disrupted them a bit. Some made major conceptual shifts, others pushed slightly upon the parameters of their beliefs.

At the outset of multicultural service learning, a majority of white, midwestern preservice teachers expressed deficit views of youth of color or in poverty. Real interactions with culturally diverse youth and adults challenged their negative stereotypes. They recognized difficult conditions of poverty, but they rarely situated problems within larger social contexts of power. Instead, they blamed parents for inadequacies in children's lives. Some white preservice teachers considered themselves "saviors" who could offer stability to children.

Many white preservice teachers moved toward more affirmative views of their community contexts. They shifted from perceptions of children as "troubled" to perceptions of children as "all alike." Recognition of commonalities was a position of respect, but it eschewed difference in favor of human universals. Inequality was seen as a matter of equal access and opportunities. Preservice teachers saw all "kids as kids" and expected that "all students have equal opportunities to learn."

Another form of affirmation was making connections between prior experiences of discrimination and realities observed in communities. Preservice teachers of color, from religious minorities, or from poverty backgrounds tended to make these linkages. For example, a Jewish preservice teacher recalled her experience with anti-Semitism to understand a racist name-calling incident at a community center. Also, a few preservice teachers with prior discriminatory life experiences defined service learning as "nothing new."

Some white preservice teachers expressed affirmative views in pragmatic terms. They honed in on making a difference through becoming a better teacher for individual youth. They planned to diversify teaching strate-gies to assist culturally diverse or low-income youth. Although they mostly perceived children's home lives from afar, they promised future sensitivity to students' life circumstances. For example, a prospective music teacher planned to eliminate costly uniforms, which might deter low-income youth from participation in choir. More diverse, sensitive teaching ostensibly allowed individuals to take advantage of educational opportunities.

Most of the preservice teachers of color and a very few white prospec-tive teachers were activists in the making. They searched for community strengths and resources, situated communities within a societal framework, and planned to advocate for equality and justice within their teaching. Multicultural service learning was part of an ongoing set of experiences that propelled them in this direction. For example, one prospective teacher of color worked as a volunteer for a Saturday Safety Fair in a subsidized housing project in addition to her service-learning commitments.

Prior life experience with cultural diversity or systemic inequality impacted preservice teachers' views. Not surprisingly, multicultural service learning, as a momentary educational intervention, rattled, but did not radically alter, preservice teachers' worldviews. Most white prospective teachers shifted from deficit, savior-oriented, charitable views to liberal views which negated stereotypes and accentuated equal worth, rights, and chances. Willingness to make changes in schools was usually limited to assurance of a more "equal playing field." Prospective teachers of color or from other minority groups made the kind of linkages that promised chal-lenges to racism and ethnocentrism in schools. A few preservice teachers, mostly those of color, operated solidly within the social change paradigm.

THEORIZING

This conceptual framework clarifies meanings made by preservice teachers related to multicultural service learning. For most preservice teachers, multicultural service learning fell short of aims for a broadly conceptualized multicultural education. It jolted awareness of culture, race, and economic adversity, but stalled prior to structural analysis of inequity. Yet, for some preservice teachers, mostly of color, the experience gener-ated deeper understandings of cultural diversity and social inequality. In light of this research, several theoretical proposals can be made: Prior life experience with cultural diversity or poverty impacts one's perceptions of multicultural service learning; preservice teachers hold paradigmatic (not continuous or progressive) views; and multicultural service learning spurs conceptual shifts that affirm a multicultural education. For the last claim, affirmation of a multicultural education can center on support for human dignity and cultural diversity but stop short of critical examination of social structures of power. Likely, multiple meanings for affirmation are held.

In this chapter, case studies of four diverse individuals stand alone as moments of meaning making, but also inform the conceptual framework and test the theoretical claims. As a caveat, data and analysis are meant to deepen understanding of service learning as part of a multicultural education, not to suggest if-then predictions, as in grounded theory (Strauss & Corbin, 1994). Three questions drive this inquiry: What meanings did preservice teachers make of their multicultural service-learning experiences? In what ways do the profiles upset or reinforce the Boyle-Baise/Sleeter conceptual framework? To what extent do the profiles support the theoretical claims?

INVESTIGATIONS

This inquiry is a companion to the research reported in Chapter 4. From a class of 24 preservice teachers, 4 were invited to serve as individual case studies. I sought a diverse subset that might represent divergent views of multicultural service learning and push conceptual and theoretical parameters. The choice of this subgroup was based on variations of criterion-based selection (LeCompte & Preissle, 1993). In the larger class, 20 preservice teachers were white, 7 male and 13 female. Four preservice teachers were of color, 2 Latino, 2 African American. I used quota sampling to identify respondents by gender and ethnicity. Anthony was a European American male, Elizabeth was a European American female, Cristina was a Mexican American female, and Natalie was an African American female. All 4 informants were of traditional college age, 2 college sophomores, 2 juniors.

I utilized a demographic survey to provide indications of diverse backgrounds. Anthony and Cristina were from small towns, Elizabeth and Natalie were from major cities. Preservice teachers' parents varied in educational attainment, and their families ranged in income level. These preservice teachers also had mixed K–12 school experiences. Three described their schooling as mostly segregated; Anthony attended predominately white schools, Cristina and Natalie attended minority-majority schools. Natalie and Elizabeth went to desegregated high schools, but racial mixing inside the schools was limited.

Scores on a pretest of ethnic identity (Ford, 1979) were another selection factor. This test correlates with Bank's (1988) five stages of ethnic identity. It has been used as a means of self-awareness for many years in

multicultural education courses at my university. Scores are shared pri-
vately with preservice teachers as a sign of their ethnic development. Most
preservice teachers score at stage 3 and a few score at stage 4 of Banks'
typology. Stage 3 is ethnic identity clarification: An individual develops
clear, positive identification with his or her own ethnic group. Stage 4 is
biethnicity: An individual possesses a healthy sense of ethnic identity and
skills to function in another ethnic culture.

Except for Elizabeth, respondents began multicultural service learning at stage 3. Elizabeth posted a score high in stage 4, which suggested a
strong sense of biethnic identification. Natalie scored in the lower end of
stage 3, which indicated some struggle with her ethnic identity. In regard
to this measure, the subgroup compared with the larger class, yet offered
some slight divergence.

These four preservice teachers agreed to complete two lengthy solo
interviews. Also, they participated in three interviews with their site-based
service-learning teams. Along with the rest of the class, they agreed to
submit their four reflective essays and final class projects to a pool of data
for this research. The four profiles were constructed from an aggregate of
this data.

Although carefully chosen, I did not have to retain a focus on these
individuals. Yet, based on early data such as first solo interviews and reflective essays, these respondents promised to illuminate the conceptual
framework and the theoretical positions in novel ways. Natalie and Cristina
perceived multicultural service learning as a trial for interracial mixing.
Since service learning is usually approached as an opportunity for white
preservice teachers to gain experience with cultural diversity, this was a new
twist to learning from service learning. Anthony approached encounters with
cultural difference with a sense of adventure. Elizabeth seemed less ethnically acute than her test of ethnic development indicated; although raised
in a racially diverse city, she experienced minimal cross-race interaction.
Commonly, white preservice teachers express uncertainty about working
with people unlike themselves; Anthony did not. Also, white preservice
teachers from culturally diverse or low-income backgrounds articulate a
stronger grasp of discrimination or inequality than did Elizabeth. Profiles of
Anthony and Elizabeth showed potential to add nuance to the framework
of preservice teacher's views of multicultural service learning.

Theoretical sampling was intended as well (LeCompte & Preissle,
1993). Since respondents differed in prior life experience, biographical
impact upon perspective possibly could be gleaned. Given the previous
studies, paradigmatic views were likely to differ by race and ethnicity.
Moreover, various conceptual changes, paradigmatic shifts, and deepened
views were likely to be observed in a racially, ethnically diverse subgroup.

A few caveats are in order. Although the profiles are based on an array of data, each profile only glimpses preservice teachers' reactions to multicultural service learning. In order to fashion more accurate portrayals, preservice teachers were invited to review and modify their profiles. In addition, the profiles are excerpted from their context. The multicultural education course and the service learning site fade into the background. Chapters 3 and 4 should be read as a couplet, as the next chapter describes field experiences for the class from which these profiles were drawn.

PROFILES

The information presented here is culled from a large body of data. The following dimensions underpin each description: previous life experience with cultural diversity and poverty; learning through service learning; and benefits of service learning.

Natalie

> I was raised in an all-black neighborhood. If we saw someone from any different culture, we'd say you're not in the right place. My church was all-black, my service-learning church is very mixed. They are so loving and caring. I'm thinking it's because when you have different races of people you start to be more open and more caring. You knock that whole image of what you used to think about people. (N.G., interview, 10/26/98)

Natalie did not experience much cultural diversity as a youth. She described her urban neighborhood as "all-black." Her elementary school was segregated, but her middle school mixed Latino, African American, and European American students. In high school, her school was desegregated through busing. As she described it: "They're not shipping the white kids from that neighborhood. They're just shipping the black kids in. It's not working out well" (interview, 10/26/98). Natalie did not experience a teacher of color until high school, then she said her attitude about school improved.

Natalie grew up in poverty, though she did not realize it until high school. Her grandmother struggled to raise Natalie and her siblings alone, after her father left and her mother died. According to Natalie, her grandmother, who had minimal formal education, focused on "moral-type raising." She was a role model in and beyond her local community; she was highly respected in her church, even among adults who grew up in the neighborhood, moved away, and then returned as church members.

Natalie's family did not want her to attend a predominately white state university (after this college year, she transferred to a racially mixed, urban campus). She described her family as "racist," particularly distrustful of white people. Since high school, Natalie tried to be "more open to all races," but this was difficult for her family. "I had more white friends than black friends. They didn't come over to my house. I had to make sure they didn't call much. I had to have more black people than white people call." Natalie bowed to peer pressure: "If you did too much with them [whites] then we didn't want to be bothered with you anymore. You were left out, like you like white people better than black people" (interview, 10/26/98).

Prior to the multicultural education class, Natalie paid little attention to other minority ethnic groups: "I never thought of Asian people. I thought they lived in their own little world." She also noted: "I see Mexicans differently. I didn't know they had so many stereotypes toward them. Wow, they have more stereotypes than we [African Americans] do" (interview 10/26/98).

Based on the advice of a high school counselor, and because her sister had preceded her to campus, Natalie chose the state over the urban university. However, she did not get along with her sister or enjoy a large campus. She decided to transfer to the urban school. "I'm transferring because I like [the urban campus]. I don't like it just because of the number of black people there. But now my family says, 'I told you so'" (interview, 10/26/98).

Natalie's multicultural service learning was done in a racially mixed church (with African American leadership). She selected a church because she was accustomed to regular attendance and worship. At this church, Natalie experienced rich, cross-cultural interaction in an affirmative atmosphere. "It was nice to see people of different races come worship together and get along together." The church climate altered her views of social class: "I can tell some of the people are not middle class, but they don't separate themselves from each other." In her home church, "people separate themselves, the middle class don't interact with people who come to church in limousines" (interview, 11/18/98). Natalie was surprised that her service-learning church was so loving and caring, and she wondered about the impact of integration: "I'm thinking it's because when you have different races you start to be more open and more caring" (interview, 10/9/98).

Natalie's community service experience "knocked" her "whole image of people" (interview, 10/26/98). On her first day at church, older white people hugged her in welcome. Natalie felt "weird." "I was more comfortable around younger white people. I did not think older white people wanted to be around black people. I don't think that way anymore" (interview, 11/18/98).

Natalie still was "confused" but "open" to the potential of racially mixed situations. She could see herself teaching a racially mixed class and helping all students become comfortable there. She pondered what it meant to help black and white students learn in different ways, yet treat them equally. She had not considered teaching in a private school, uncomfortable with large numbers of white students and uncertain officials would hire her. Now, she was willing to teach anywhere.

Natalie felt she received more from her community service site than she gave to it. She felt she was invited into and became part of the congregation. For Natalie, multicultural service learning prompted self-realizations: "I really think differently about people of all colors. I am upset with myself for the way I used to view others because of their race or culture" (essay, 11/28/98). It confirmed teaching as her career choice: "I realize I feel good when I am around children" (essay, 10/31/98). And, it boosted her self-confidence: "I am more self-confident about going out in public and being too nervous to say or do things" (essay, 11/28/98).

Anthony

> It's [service learning] been a real eye-opener. Coming from a small country town and going into an African American church. It's really fun to meet different people. It's kind of cool to get out and see how everybody's point of view is different, and how people can come together and solve a problem. It's going to make me a better teacher, more well-rounded. It's going to make me a more diverse human being. (A.S., interview, 12/7/98)

Anthony thought a wide variety of experiences, good and bad, made him a better teacher. Anthony's mother was a high school graduate, his father earned a graduate degree. He was the oldest of three brothers, from a small in-state town. His background was homogeneous; his high school had "500 white kids and that was it" (interview, 10/28/98). Anthony was a practicing Catholic. He often compared his service learning at a racially mixed, nondenominational church to his customary religious life. Anthony had participated in service efforts in high school. As part of school clubs, he gave Christmas baskets to families in poverty. He had viewed destitute conditions and was uncomfortable with them. He was mollified by the seeming "good spirits" of most low-income families.

Anthony considered himself "outgoing and open to things that are different and adventuresome" (essay, 10/28/98). Just prior to the semester of multicultural service learning, Anthony worked as a summer camp counselor for "at-risk" urban Latino youth. "Coming from Indiana," he expected "a bunch of hellions" who would "bring knives to camp" and "fight all the time." Instead, youth respected the counselors and smuggled only candy into the camp. Anthony knew that these seventh and eighth graders lived in poverty and had relatives in gangs, yet he saw them as kids who loved to play soccer and other games like "normal" kids (interview, 10/28/98).

Anthony "never really thought about the black community" because he "never grew up in one." He viewed service learning as an "eye-opening exposure" to difference. For example, "going to a church predominately of African Americans never crossed my mind. People my age are never exposed to this different style of doing things" (essay, 12/2/98). Anthony did not feel comfortable "just coming out and asking questions." He preferred to observe actions, then rethink the moment. This stance seemed to keep him on the "exposure" or surface level of his "adventures," satisfied with knowledge of cultural artifacts. For example, at camp he noticed that Latino youth cleaned their shoes nightly and added hot sauce to most foods. He did not push further to glean reasons for this behavior from inside the group itself.

Anthony welcomed exposure to difference as something "fun" and "cool." He had "made new friends from different ethnic groups, learned more about the community, and really had a good time" (essay, 10/7/98). He enjoyed the "warmth" and "compassion" of church members and the "enthusiasm" of church services. He found his own Catholic upbringing "boring," "monotone," and distant in comparison. Personally, church attendance was a "big, big change for me, a change I was ready for" (essay, 10/7/98).

In regard to poverty-stricken families, Anthony thought teachers should treat students the "same as kids who are well-off," but "in the back of your mind know where they are coming from" (interview, 12/7/98). He struggled to balance differences related to living conditions with similarities based upon the inherent worth of all human beings.

Multicultural service learning was deemed beneficial by Anthony: He was interested in learning more about cultural difference—he liked to try "something new" (interview, 12/7/98). If he could learn something new and provide some benefit to others, all the better. Anthony articulated his growth in the following way: "I have seen and felt some changes. Changes in the way I look at people of color and changes within myself." He saw

African American adults who were "deeply involved" in church studies, "extremely supportive" of their children's learning, "so proud, positive, and caring" (essay, 10/2/98). He found himself more willing to "try things," to become a "more well-rounded" person; for example, he was willing to enter another situation where he was in the minority (interview, 12/7/98). Anthony saw multicultural service learning as an opportunity to become a "more diverse person" and "a better teacher," someone who could handle a range of people and situations encountered in the classroom. Anthony hoped to translate church members' enthusiasm and support for children's learning to his future classroom.

Elizabeth

> I grew up in a wealthy suburb outside St. Louis and have never experienced poverty. This experience opened my mind. It has helped me understand that although we may all look alike on the outside, the differences between us are incredible. [But] the kids [at Head Start] are cheerful and want to learn just as much as any other child. (E.C., essay, 10/7/98)

Elizabeth moved around some, but grew up primarily in an upper-income suburb of St. Louis. Her mother earned a college degree, her father a graduate degree. In her family, Italian customs were passed down from immigrant grandparents. Elizabeth's ethnic identity centered around memories of special holiday meals. She did not recall many cross-cultural youthful experiences.

During Elizabeth's youth, St. Louis was divided racially and economically by county-city lines. Middle- and upper-class "collar" counties tended to be white; urban, low-income neighborhoods tended to be black. In order to desegregate, city kids were bused out to the counties, but county kids were not bused into the city. Inside junior and senior high schools, resegregation occurred. According to Elizabeth, "you had your own set of friends, you weren't forced to be friends with others" (interview, 10/27/98). Elizabeth recalled two good African American friends from her elementary school: They were welcome in her home, but she was not allowed to visit their homes in the city. In junior and senior high school, she thought black, city students "must be different or we would have hung out" (interview, 12/9/98). Her school focused on "white history." Students could voluntarily attend a lecture about black history, but few white students did.

Elizabeth was part of an experimental, community service class as a high school senior. Students visited elderly residents of nursing homes, developed a "disabilities awareness day" for fellow students, and served in a soup kitchen on Thanksgiving. She also worked as a camp counselor prior to college. As part of her job, she chaperoned 10-year-olds as they worked in a mission for homeless men. The shelter was in a "very, very bad part of St. Louis." Elizabeth was startled to realize that "people really lived like this" (interview, 10/27/98).

When Elizabeth went to Head Start for her multicultural service learning, she struggled with understandings of poverty. She wrote: "At the beginning I felt very sorry for the children. I wanted to rescue them and give them things they could not afford." She learned, however, "how happy these children really are. They do not have privileges in life, but that has not hindered their happiness" (essay, 11/28/98). Elizabeth did not think children even considered the "money aspect of things" (interview, 12/9/98). She noticed that "they are no different than any other child. They are in Head Start. That's the only thing that sets them apart" (interview, 9/29/98). She focused her energies on "what was happening in the classroom, not what was going on in their lives, because I knew the children were happy" (essay, 11/28/98). Service learning upset a "horrible picture" in Elizabeth's mind of children in poverty. She replaced deficit views of the children with perceptions of their "normality."

The experience was "mind-opening" (essay, 10/21/98) in other ways as well. Based on media coverage, Elizabeth anticipated small-town racism. Instead, children played easily across racial lines and did not seem to notice race at all. She also anticipated that kids in poverty would be of color. Instead, most students were white. Elizabeth found children more "blunt" (in need of reminders to say please and thank you) and more independent than children in her neighborhood.

Elizabeth valued multicultural service learning as an opportunity to become a better teacher and person. She accompanied her Head Start teacher on home visits. She observed low-income parents as they participated in Head Start programs. Elizabeth began to think that, like upper- and middle-class parents, low-income parents wanted the best education for their children. In the Head Start classroom, Elizabeth noticed (and praised) attention to multiple ways of learning and to language diversity (a few words were posted in dual languages). Generally though, kids were treated the same, as just kids, a stance Elizabeth found entirely appropriate.

Elizabeth felt she gave to and received from her service site. As a college student, she served as a role model for the children. In return, "this experience is giving me ideas for handling my own classroom and also ideas for my curriculum" (essay, 11/11/98). Elizabeth saw all children similarly: "Just because they are in a different income bracket does not change the child, they have the same needs, wants, and desires as other children." She realized that "teaching them all the same isn't the answer" (interview,

12/9/98). Instead, she planned to know each child and correlate her teaching methods to his or her learning preferences.

Multicultural service learning was "mind-opening, a lot of stereotypes I had going in, I don't have anymore." For example, she had thought that "if a child was living in government housing, the parents probably don't care about their child's education." Now, she realized "their children are their first priority" (interview, 12/9/98). As a teacher, she would not jump to conclusions about "good" parenting.

Cristina

At first I thought only my way was correct. I never tried to associate with white people. I never tried to be their friend, or even get to know them. Now, I see it in a whole different way. I try to think of different views. I want my students to see not only one way, but in different views. (C.R., interview, 12/4/98)

Cristina came from a family of six, loved being around children, and had always wanted to be a teacher. She grew up in East Chicago, in a Latino and black neighborhood. Her mother finished eighth grade, and her father finished high school. Her parents were raised Catholic, but changed to a Pentecostal faith. Cristina attended a Pentecostal church, with Mexican and Puerto Rican parishioners. She started school speaking Spanish. In her hometown, racism toward whites was common: "We always thought white people were stuck-up and too rich" (interview, 10/28/98). As a child, Cristina did not have any white friends. However, she enjoyed friendships with Hispanic and black youth.

In her senior year of high school, Cristina's high grades spurred her counselor to encourage attendance at the state university. During her early days on campus, Cristina was uncertain how to act around white classmates, who constituted the majority of students. She was startled to find herself a lone person of color in many classes. She thought there was no way to compare herself to her white counterparts. Yet, as she got acquainted with her white classmates, she found more similarities than she had expected. For example, she learned that, like herself, some white students felt uncomfortable with racial diversity or overwhelmed by a large campus.

Cristina did not do community service work prior to college. The year before this multicultural education class, she served as a tutor for an elementary school in a local, low-income neighborhood. The service learning experience was short, just three visits. Cristina disclaimed it as a valuable learning experience.

As a significant aspect of her multicultural service learning experience, Cristina noticed racial divides. Before she arrived at Boys and Girls Club, she worried: "What if the white kids do not want to play with me?" (essay, 11/28/98). On site, she recognized that a group of black boys did not associate with white children. One black youth gravitated toward her. He felt "comfortable because I was like one of his people" (essay, 10/20/98). He explained that he felt more at ease playing with his own group. Cristina counseled the boy that "white kids are not bad people" (essay, 10/20/98). Additionally, a white girl told Cristina that she did not play with black kids because they refused to play with her. The girl decided that all black people were mean. Cristina countered this statement with her own positive life experiences. These encounters helped Cristina realize that minority youth preferred their own company, white children learned prejudice in childhood, and she was able to "get along with white kids as well as black kids." She planned to utilize this latter strength to "keep my class equal" (interview, 12/4/98).

Cristina considered her income level "the same" as that of the youth at Boys and Girls Club. She did not classify kids as low-income, she saw them as "regular" kids. She was "amused" that a good number of parents or relatives attended the Halloween party with their children. Cristina did not downgrade parents who did not attend: "Other parents are not able to show up because of personal problems or work. We cannot judge those parents because we are not in their footsteps on an everyday basis" (essay, 11/28/98). Children's delight in their parents' participation, spurred Cristina to consider avenues for parental involvement in her future classroom.

Cristina looked at multicultural service learning pragmatically, as how it helped her become a better teacher. She became more comfortable around a diverse mix of children. She gained insight into different learning modes. She intended to teach every student, not just the one "who knows how to catch on real quick." She realized that "black and white kids have struggles in school." As she tutored, she practiced teaching to students' "different minds" (interview, 10/28/98). She also realized her special power to communicate with youth of color: "Minorities are able to communicate more with their own people" (interview, 12/4/98). Multicultural service learning motivated Cristina to graduate and become a teacher responsive to cultural diversity.

Cristina felt amiable toward her cross-race service learning team. She became friends with her white classmates: "I don't see them as a color any more." This realization extended to all whites, not just to her service learning team. Cristina began to see whites as individuals, "as a person, as who they are." She hoped to teach a positive view of difference to her future students: "I want my students to see not only one way, but in different views" (interview, 12/4/98).

MAKING MEANING

What meanings did preservice teachers make of their multicultural service learning experiences? In what ways do the profiles disturb or strengthen the conceptual framework? To what extent do profiles support the theoretical propositions?

Meanings

These profiles are four individual portrayals. I fear to overgeneralize from them. Yet, the profiles illuminate multicultural service learning, particularly its perception among prospective teachers with divergent life experiences. At the risk of being overly simplistic, I suggest the following representation. If I envision these four profiles in relation to a Venn diagram, Anthony and Elizabeth's views, as white, middle-class preservice teachers, are located in one circle. Natalie and Cristina's perspectives, as future teachers of color from low-income to working-class backgrounds, are located in another. Their ideas about becoming a better teacher overlap.

Although their backgrounds differ in several ways (i.e., small town vs. city origins, segregated vs. desegregated high schools, middle- vs. upper-class families), Anthony and Elizabeth articulate similar perspectives. Both enter multicultural service learning with little understanding of cultural diversity or poverty. Although Elizabeth lived in the midst of racial desegregation, it barely touched her life. Anthony and Elizabeth see poverty from afar and grasp it as general destitution. Their prior experience with difference is charitable in nature: work in a soup kitchen, visit a mission, or deliver Christmas baskets. Elizabeth stands ready to rescue children from poverty situations.

Anthony and Elizabeth's outlooks shift, from deficit to affirmative views. They question their stereotypes; for example, Anthony realizes that adolescent Latino campers are not the violent gang members he expected. Anthony and Elizabeth have nagging notions that kids' lives are not normal, but, to them, youth are unaware of bias or adversity—they are just happy. As they elevate their regard for children unlike themselves, Anthony and Elizabeth disclaim difference. Once at this point, it is difficult to reclaim children's adverse life conditions.

Kozol (2000) refers to the dualism between universal humanness and varied life situations in his book *Ordinary Resurrections*:

> It is true that the conditions of their lives are different . . . their breathing problems and the absence of so many of their fathers in the prison system being two of the most obvious distinctions, but the ordinary things they long for,

and the things they find funny, and the infinite variety of things they dream of, and the games they play . . . are not as different as the world seems to believe from what most other children in this land enjoy, or dream of. (p. 118)

Anthony and Elizabeth struggle to grasp this dualism. They mistake kids' resiliency, their making the best of tough situations, as undiluted happiness.

Anthony and Elizabeth are open-minded, willing to flex their views. They are buoyed by welcoming service-learning environments. They are included in ongoing communities where members respect one another and share common aims. They also build community, in that they develop linkages with their service-learning sites. Anthony actually makes good friends and has a good time. Elizabeth recognizes that her hope for children's educational achievement also is held by parents struggling with poverty.

Anthony and Elizabeth consider their experiences good practice for their future teaching. Both plan to alter their pedagogy, either with more options for learning or with greater enthusiasm for teaching. Elizabeth seems to think of class management in deficit terms, as learning to handle children (supposedly in need of control). Both intend to treat students alike, with some regard (vaguely defined) for their difficult home lives. Elizabeth repudiates prior judgments of parents or students as uncaring or unable.

Elizabeth and Anthony articulate views of service learning that reflect their status in dominant racial and social groups. Both enter multicultural service learning with charitable outlooks based on deficit views. Both shift conceptually to liberal notions of equality—all kids are alike, kids of color or in poverty are "normal." To them, better teaching means attending to children's learning preferences in order to increase their opportunities to learn. Equality means either "not seeing" difference, as Elizabeth intends, or "celebrating diversity," as Anthony hopes. These interpretations are standard fare for the "haves" in society; society is based on merit—given hard work, everyone has an equal chance to succeed. Elizabeth's prior experience in desegregated schools did not seem to rattle this view. Anthony and Elizabeth's profiles point up the need for structural analyses of discrimination and oppression as part of multicultural service learning.

Natalie and Cristina also come to multicultural service learning from segregated backgrounds, but grasp it in terms of racism instead of geography (I live here, "they" live there). They see color as part of their daily service-learning activities, contrary to Elizabeth's difference-blind stance or Anthony's tendency to exoticize race. They come to service learning with social change outlooks. They make connections between discriminatory life experiences and course concepts or service-learning events. For example, Natalie recognizes that Mexican Americans face racism, similar to her own racial-ethnic group. Natalie and Cristina situate their experiences within larger societal relations of power. For example, Natalie is quite aware of ostracism related to acting too white. Both look to family and church as resources in low-income neighborhoods.

Natalie and Cristina do not shift from one paradigm to another, but their perceptions of racism and integration transform. Natalie says multicultural service learning "knocked her whole image of people." She seems to disrupt her image of racial divides. Both women become more comfortable in racially mixed situations. For Cristina, increased ease with whites seems part of an ongoing process. For Natalie, the moment of modification seems to lie within service learning, in an unexpected welcome from older adult, white church members. Natalie and Cristina move toward heightened acceptance of integration and toward more pluralistic views.

Not surprisingly, given that preservice teachers were just beginning their teacher education program and that service learning was a field experience for a teacher education class, the pragmatic aim of becoming a better teacher resonated through all the profiles. However, becoming a better teacher carried different connotations, again related to racial or ethnic group. Better teaching for Natalie and Cristina meant diversified teaching techniques, but also much more. It meant imagining work in a culturally mixed situation and figuring out how to help youth grapple with cultural diversity and racism. Also, multicultural service learning endorsed their value as future teachers of color. They realized they could make a difference in the lives of their future students of color.

Natalie and Cristina alert service-learning practitioners to potential uneasiness, among preservice teachers of color, about working with white cohorts or clientele. Their interpretations further accentuate the need to situate service-learning experiences within a larger societal framework. Natalie and Cristina need to understand their views of and discomfort with white people as part of racial and ethnic discrimination and oppression. They must grapple with the potential of and limits for cross-race friendship to spur social change. Their cases demonstrate that critical pedagogy, as part of a broadly conceptualized multicultural education, is needed to help scrutinize service-learning field experiences.

Conceptual Framework

Data from this subgroup of preservice teachers generally braces the conceptual framework detailed earlier (i.e., deficit, affirmative, pragmatic, and activist views). Although these perceptions cannot be attributed solely to multicultural service learning, according to preservice teachers' self-analyses, conceptual shifts and alterations of the following types occurred.

All four preservice teachers held deficit views. Similar to the studies summarized at the outset of this chapter, white prospective teachers initially held negative stereotypes of youth of color or in poverty. The perspectives of the preservice teachers of color add a new wrinkle to the conceptual framework. They, too, came to multicultural service learning with negative perceptions, but of white people. Natalie also expresses ignorance of other ethnic minority groups (e.g., Asian Americans). All four preservice teachers articulated reservations about racial or ethnic groups with whom they had little direct contact as youths.

The entire subgroup turned toward more affirmative perceptions of cultural difference during multicultural service learning. White preservice teachers shifted from views of children of color or in poverty as "hellions" who lived "horrible" lives to children who were "happy" and "normal." Preservice teachers of color modified their views of whites as "stuck-up" and "unapproachable" to whites as individuals and welcoming.

As in the Boyle-Baise/Sleeter framework, Natalie and Cristina, prospective teachers of color, made connections between their earlier experiences of discrimination and their current service-learning realities. However, Anthony and Elizabeth, white preservice teachers, made connections too; they watched kids play and found them as "normal" as kids from their own cultural-social groups. Making connections was paradigmatically based; it emerged from two different perspectives. From a community-building (social change) position, it meant deepened understanding of bias or oppression. From a liberal position, it meant elevated regard for culturally diverse or poor children—as kids "just like us."

A pragmatic orientation to becoming a better teacher was expressed by all four preservice teachers, not just white preservice teachers, as in the conceptual framework. In these cases, white preservice teachers defined school reform in liberal terms, as "add-ons" that amplified opportunities to learn. Preservice teachers of color approached teaching as change makers, ready to alter their teaching to affirm racial-ethnic heterogeneity and equality.

Natalie and Cristina were activists in the making. They recognized assets in low-income communities, they perceived themselves as resources for students of color, they understood racism, and they committed to antiracist teaching. To some extent, Anthony unsettled this framework. He was willing to broaden his mind through placement in situations where he is in the minority. His readiness to face likely discomfort tilted toward activism. Certainly, this willingness to participate in venues beyond one's comfort zone is something to be cultivated during multicultural service learning and beyond, as a suggestion for continued growth.

These cases inform the Boyle-Baise/Sleeter conceptual framework. For the most part, categories are reinforced, but also they are amplified. The amplifications stem from the interpretation of meaning making from paradigmatic, as well as categorical positions. The conceptual framework was posed prior to my arguments for paradigmatic perspectives. The categories of the former do not match exactly the orientations of the latter. The conceptual framework is enveloped by the broader, ideologic stances. As a result, categories of meaning can be understood more subtly. For example, themes of "making connections" and "becoming a better teacher" cross paradigms and are interpreted differently within the liberal (civic education) or the community-building (social change) position.

Theoretical Propositions

Prior life experience, or biography, matters. Who one is impacts what one sees and does. Natalie and Cristina, preservice teachers of color, demonstrate sensitivity to racial concerns. Yet, like white students who grow up in segregated milieus, they struggle with deficit notions of groups other than their own. They gravitate toward youth of color, but multicultural service learning also generates comfort within racially mixed situations. Anthony and Elizabeth, white preservice teachers from segregated backgrounds, express negative views of people of color or in poverty. Multicultural service learning is, for them, an invitation to respect and value people different from themselves. For both groups, multicultural service learning provides a public space to work through and discount deficit notions.

In these cases, there is little sense of movement along a continuum from a personal connection with someone in need to a grasp of social problems, to a concern for societal justice. Rather, this group seems grounded in several paradigms, with some conceptual shifting from one stance to another. Anthony and Elizabeth seem to shift from charitable to liberal or civic education views. They move from thoughts of rescue to plans for teaching that will help all children learn. Natalie and Cristina seem to delve deeper into the community-building (social change) paradigm, assisted by friendly, racially mixed, service-learning sites. They ponder ways to affirm cultural diversity: to increase comfort in mixed-race classes, to foster positive cross-group relations, and to mitigate educational struggles for all students. Their views align with a broadly conceptualized multicultural education, as outlined in Chapter 1.

Multicultural service learning augments multicultural education, albeit not as broadly as intended in some cases. Liberal or civic education standpoints are a double-edged sword: Recognition of equal worth opens the door to excellent education for all students; yet, equality as sameness can impede learning for a diverse range of students. As noted in Chapter 2, liberal perspectives often gloss over structural problems and focus instead on chances for individual improvement. The practice of diverse teaching strategies likely will benefit many students. However, multicultural education is reduced, in this interpretation, to a benign, uncritical form. Multicultural service learning needs to be carefully planned to exemplify antiracist education, critical pedagogy, and education for social justice (as described in Chapter 1).

MULTICULTURAL SERVICE LEARNING: IDEAL TO REAL

How do these profiles inform practice for multicultural service learning? Most research on community-based service learning, as part of multicultural education or social foundation courses, focuses on white prospective teachers (e.g., Dunlap, 1998; Fuller, 1998; O'Grady & Chappell, 2000; Sleeter, 1995; Tellez et al., 1995). These profiles depict the standpoints of prospective teachers of color and their white counterparts; they inform multicultural service learning from plural perspectives.

Deficit views of groups other than one's own should be interrogated as part of multicultural service learning. Examinations should not be confined to white racism, but delve into bias against whites as well. Distinctive paradigms, and who usually holds which and why, should also be taught. Puzzling through divergent perspectives can assist preservice teachers in locating and grappling with their own views. Liberal orientations should be thickened or deepened to support a broadly conceptualized multicultural education. Notions of equal opportunity should be problematized. Questions about equal opportunity for whom and under what circumstances should be raised.

Tenets of a broadly conceptualized multicultural education should be stressed. Systemic racism and other root causes for inequality especially deserve attention. To this end, praxis, as action based on critical reflection, is meaningful for multicultural service learning. Reflective discussions should probe systemic bases for everyday problems. Multicultural service learning offers authentic opportunities to apply the ends of critique, to rethink daily realities in ways that are antiracist, prodifference, and socially just.

As course instructor, I impacted the perceptions of these preservice teachers. I approached service learning as fundamental to the process of becoming a multicultural person and teacher (as described in Chapter 1).

The emphasis on becoming a better teacher that crossed these profiles sprang from the multicultural education course. I did not intend, however, for multicultural teaching to be defined narrowly as teaching strategies or as curricular add-ons.

The class from which these profiles were developed read and reviewed a novel about life in a low-income Chicago neighborhood, *There Are No Children Here* (Kotlowitz, 1991). In this journalistic account, real-life hopes, dreams, and fears of two brothers are chronicled as they struggle to survive in a dilapidated, violence-prone, housing project and learn in underfunded city schools. As an aspect of their review, preservice teachers studied government responses to violence and poverty, and resourcefulness in families and communities. Preservice teachers' book reviews did not necessarily translate to multicultural service learning. It was a case of disconnected aims and ends (as put forth in Chapter 2). While we examined societal aspects of poverty in class, many preservice teachers focused on programmatic aid to individuals, like tutoring, in the field. I wrongly expected prospective teachers to leap from helping children with homework to understanding societal conditions that impacted children's lives. Instead, preservice teachers tended to find the novel and the service learning thought provoking and beneficial, but loosely connected—a mismatch, if you will.

In the next chapter, prospective teachers, like those profiled, are followed into the field, inside their community-based, service-learning experiences. Readers can glimpse what really happened there and consider the extent to which the real matched the ideal for multicultural service learning. A reminder: This book represents an ongoing journey toward "shared control" as a watchword for multicultural service learning. These profiles and the field study reported in the next chapter were drawn from the same class at the same moment in time. They illustrate one point on my journey. What did and did not happen in this "round" of multicultural service learning spurred the rethinking that lead to shared control, the emphasis of Chapters 5 and 6.

CHAPTER 4

What Really Happens?
A Look Inside Multicultural
Service Learning

MARILYNNE BOYLE-BAISE
with JAMES KILBANE

What really happens in multicultural service learning? How do its intentions actually play out in the field, as preservice teachers serve and learn
in community organizations? In this chapter, we investigate one cycle of
service learning. We detail what happened during actual events of service
learning and ponder the extent to which field experiences assisted preservice
teachers in becoming multicultural people and educators. As noted in
Chapter 1, Nieto (2000) claims that becoming a multicultural teacher
means first becoming a multicultural person. To that end, preservice
teachers need to question their own racism and biases, learn more about
cultural diversity and poverty, and grapple with realities from multiple perspectives. This process of becoming demands a willingness to look within,
to reflect upon one's past and present views, to root out false assumptions,
and to reeducate oneself in ways that affirm cultural difference and support educational equality and equity.

As put forth in Chapter 1, community-based learning in culturally
diverse or low-income neighborhoods (and in the organizations that serve
them) can prompt and sustain such self-reflection and personal transformation. It can push preservice teachers outside their comfort zones into
spaces where new realizations are possible. It can emotionally jolt preservice
teachers' attention to real-life conditions of diversity, adversity, and ineq-

This chapter originally appeared in the *Michigan Journal of Community Service Learning, 7*,
54–64 (*www.umich.edu/'ocsl/MJCSL*), and appears here with permission of the editor.

uity. It can help preservice teachers perceive children as other than students in the classroom, as community and family members, and as youngsters with talents, lifeways, and concerns of their own. It can prod preservice teachers to recognize assets in communities other than their own and help them imagine connections between children's home lives and school days (e.g., Mahan et al., 1983; Sleeter, 2000). These expectations are lofty. Nevertheless, the profiles of preservice teachers presented in Chapter 3 suggest at least partial realization of them.

The problem is that little is known about how multicultural service learning actually works. How does it propel (or not propel) self-study and personal change? Several studies, based on self-reports of preservice teachers (journals, reflective essays, and interviews), portray the influences of multicultural service learning quite positively: Service learning increases awareness and acceptance of cultural diversity (Boyle-Baise, 1998; Sleeter, 1995; Tellez et al., 1995), challenges prejudicial, stereotypical beliefs (Fuller, 1998; O'Grady, 1997; Seigel, cited in Wade, 1998), develops more complex understandings of institutional racism (O'Grady & Chappell, 2000; Vadeboncoeur, Rahm, Aguilera, & LeCompte, 1996), and heightens commitment to teach diverse youth, particularly for European American preservice teachers (Fuller, 1998; Tellez et al., 1995). Unfortunately, little observational information underscores or refutes these reports. There is a need to determine what actually occurs during service learning to unsettle and recast preservice teacher's perspectives.

What really happens in service learning experiences that is pertinent to multicultural teacher education? What do preservice teachers do that supports or limits reconsideration of Eurocentric worldviews? Do certain experiences spur self-examination? Are there constraints to the learning process? Are there ways that experiences can be altered to motivate cultural and social insights and critique? In this chapter, we explore what happened in the field and what meanings preservice teachers made of their experiences.

THE COURSE AND THE SERVICE

A few clarifications of the context for this study are in order. Multicultural service learning was a companion field experience for a multicultural education course, intended to deepen the course, but not the whole of it. For the course, multicultural education was defined as the development of cultural knowledge and insights as well as the examination of social and cultural dynamics of power (Sleeter & Grant, 1999). Multicultural service learning was utilized as a vehicle to connect preservice teachers with culturally diverse or low-income communities and to learn from them. Aims for multicultural service learning included building cross-group relations, disrupting stereotypes, gaining awareness of community resources and problems, and learning to work positively with diverse youth.

Prior to the fall semester, six community organizations that served culturally diverse or low-income youth were invited to participate in service learning. Service sites included a historically black church, a church mixed by race and social class, two community centers, two girl scout troops for "at-risk" girls, and Head Start. Sites were chosen because they fostered a self-help, rather than a compensatory, ethic. Only one organization had not worked before with Lynne Boyle-Baise on service learning. Mixed-race inquiry teams of three to five preservice teachers were placed and worked together at each site.

Leaders (often directors) of these organizations attended an orientation lunch with us in August. We discussed aims for multicultural teacher education and for community service learning, considered ways prospective teachers might serve and learn in the field, and determined our roles in the upcoming project. We asked community leaders to explain local contexts to preservice teachers, suggest tasks for them, monitor their learning, and challenge their stereotypes. Leaders' requests for service included tutoring, teaching small groups, and assisting recreational programs. They agreed to encourage preservice teachers to attend and help organize site events and to foster acquaintance with youth, adults, and families at their sites.

In-class reflection about community experiences occurred biweekly. Preservice teachers wrote four reflective essays, and often discussion questions were drawn from them. We selected topics because of their general significance to multicultural education and their reiteration across essays. Topics included problems parents face in selecting after-school care, assumptions underlying the *at-risk* label, discipline norms across race or ethnic groups, and social conditions that cause poverty. The essays and discussions served as windows to preservice teachers' perceptions of the field, and they provided key opportunities to debunk stereotypes and question social conditions. In cases where questions were linked intimately to particular sites, preservice teachers were asked to seek advice from their community leaders. An African American parent, active in local community affairs and a liaison for one of the service-learning sites, participated in two reflective sessions and contributed her unique points of view.

Other class activities were intended to correlate community service learning and multicultural education in ways that augmented both. As examples, preservice teachers participated in Bafa Bafa, a simulation of cross-cultural differences and misunderstandings. They read *There Are No Children Here* (Kotlowitz, 1991), an account of life in a Chicago housing project, and considered the impact of violence, government intransigence, and underfunded schools on this community. Then, preservice teachers utilized this analysis to probe conditions in their service-learning sites. They also conducted ethnographic, mini-inquiries called Why?-Studies (based on Sleeter, 1995), in which teams investigated site-generated questions such as Why is the black church important for black children? and Why is the Girl Scouts important to "at-risk" girls in our county? An alternative project was the development of small curriculum units pertinent to youth at sites served. As examples, one team read fairy tales, then helped children at a community center analyze the stories for racism and sexism. Another team helped youth learn numbers and colors in Spanish, utilizing the bilingualism of one team member.

THE STUDY

This chapter describes a qualitative, interpretive case study that utilized ethnographic techniques. This case offers one of the few glimpses of what happens and what preservice teachers think about it in investigations of community service learning. In this section, the nature of the study is outlined. Details of sampling, data collection, and data analysis are provided for researchers in Appendix A.

The study took place at a large, predominately white, research university, located in a small midwestern town that was dominated by the university. Town and gown distinctions existed, particularly between local working-class citizens and highly educated university personnel. The study was located primarily in a geographically isolated, low-income part of town known as "the hill." However, one church site was situated on the periphery of this area and served people for miles around.

At the time of this study, Boyle-Baise had worked with social service organizations and churches in this area for 3 years. Far more important than geographic location was the population served. The six community service sites served culturally diverse or low-income youth and adults. These organizations offered preservice teachers sustained contact and potential acquaintance with a range of diverse people.

Preservice teachers offered their service and time to these organizations. In return, adults and children in the community welcomed and befriended the preservice teachers and taught them about themselves. The study was completed during the academic year 1998–99, but most of the information was collected during the fall semester of 1998.

The case study focused on 24 preservice teachers. The profiles in Chapter 3 were drawn from this group. As previously noted, 20 preservice teachers were white: 7 males and 13 females. Four women were of color: 2 Latinas and 2 African Americans. All but 2 preservice teachers were in-state students, most from small- or middle-size towns. Most described their neighborhoods as middle-income, although several preservice teachers grew-up in high-income or low-income situations. Most white preservice teachers had minimal direct experience with cultural diversity or poverty.

Jim Kilbane conducted the interviews and observations. Lynne Boyle-Baise taught the multicultural course. Boyle-Baise's participation in the study was disclosed fully, but described as secondary to her teaching role. We practiced a hands-off orientation to the field. Once the service learning commenced, directors of community organizations had complete discretion over activities and supervision.

Kilbane was in the field several days a week. In all, he made 33 site visits. Usually, he stayed for several hours at each site, through a complete cycle of activities. Preservice teachers were interviewed three times in small groups, with their service-learning teams. Organization directors were interviewed after the service experience. Field notes were taken during reflective class discussions. Written assignments also formed part of our database.

We met weekly to contemplate the field data. What puzzled us most were differences between preservice teachers' expressions of serious self-assessment and seemingly limited field activities. This potential gap cropped up continually in our discussions and became a key question for our investigations.

ROLES AND PERSPECTIVES

In relation to multicultural service learning, preservice teacher's roles and perspectives fell into several categories. These groupings are described separately, although their borders were fuzzy and overlapping. Factors that influenced preservice teachers' views and actions are discussed in relation to the several roles and perspectives.

Playing It Safe

To their credit, most preservice teachers did not hesitate to become involved. They did not sit back and observe, but jumped right in, eager for the experience. Yet, overwhelmingly, they were concerned with "fitting in." Early on, service was marked by accommodation to site routines. Preservice teachers played it safe; they did not stand out, they were timely, polite, and obliging. Involvement at the multiracial church exemplified safe interaction. Preservice teachers clapped and swayed during the service, but did not sing or call back to the pastor's remarks with the rest of the congregation. Preservice teachers participated just enough to fit in.

There seemed to be several safe types of interactions. One safe interaction was to stay focused on the task at hand. For example, when preservice teachers tutored at the Boys and Girls Club, they kept the children focused on doing homework. The focusing was evident across gender, but was more pronounced with the male at the site. The females were more apt to talk casually with students before returning to homework. "Task talk" extended to mentoring situations where preservice teachers played the role of big brother or sister. The conversation centered on the activity at hand: a discussion about plays in a touch football game; a question about the design of an art project. Conversation about homes, families, and life outside the center occurred, but it was uncommon. Task talk constrained chances for cross-cultural learning.

A second safe interaction was to keep comments to the students positive. As examples, during the reading program at the community center a preservice teacher coaxed a young man to read by saying, "You read better than I" (J.K., field notes, 11/11/98). At Head Start, praise was a common response for almost everything children did, from sitting nicely at the lunch table to picking up toys. At Girl Scouts, a preservice teacher told scouts who worked on a badge, "You guys got your stuff done really fast, that's great" (E.W., field notes, 10/19/98), even though the scouts were done early because they had not done as much as expected. Negative comments were rare, unless physical safety was a concern. Then, preservice teachers restrained children from unsafe actions.

A third safe interaction was to respond to youth, rather than to initiate interactions. Preservice teachers listened actively to children; rarely, however, did they probe for further information. Over time, preservice teachers especially females, took more initiative. Although some preservice teachers initiated informal conversations with youth and others attended parent meetings, most continued to describe their activities as "fitting into" the status quo.

Why did preservice teachers play it safe? For some, caution indicated uncertainty, especially about cross-cultural interactions. In a reflective essay, one white male wrote:

> When I first set foot in the African Methodist Episcopal Church, I was unsure of what to expect. I felt like an ambassador and an invader at the same time. I wanted to make a good impression and I was unsure how I would fit in. . . . Before a word was spoken, I learned a valuable piece of information. It is intimi-

dating to walk into a place where you are the minority. (C.S., essay 10/7/98)

While it is natural to be anxious about novel situations, for some white preservice teachers service learning was a powerful encounter with difference. For them, the outward appearance of compliant service work often masked internal struggle and reassessment.

Another reason for playing it safe was that it was the easy thing to do. One white female described her feelings this way: "It was my long day. I thought kids will get off school and be obnoxious. Then, it was actually fun, you get to play with them, it doesn't take a lot of brain activity. You're just hanging out with them" (J.F., interview, 9/29/98). Another white male preservice teacher expressed this view as participation in a "community service baby-sitting service" (M.H., interview, 9/29/98). For preservice teachers like these, service learning was a no-brainer opportunity to interact with children.

Playing it safe was expected by some community leaders, but disrupted by others. For example, one pastor praised preservice teachers as "really cordial," "they fit right in," and "I had no complaints" (W.M., interview, 2/18/99). Friendly adjustment to site routines translated to a "good volunteer" or a "polite visitor." Three sites exhibited these expectations: preservice teachers assisted in Sunday School, fit into a tutoring program, or served as a teacher's aide. At three other sites more leadership was encouraged: preservice teachers took charge of an Eager Reader's program, organized a Hallelujah party (a church-sponsored alternative to Halloween), and led a Girl Scout troop meeting. Some preservice teachers attended site events, including parent and board meetings, but tended to play it safe as silent observers.

The extent and nature of on-site guidance seemed to impact playing it safe. All of the community leaders offered orientations to their organizations. At most sites, however, there was minimal guidance beyond these meetings. One pastor took a laissez-faire approach; he wanted preservice teachers to feel free to assist in way they chose, and he accepted their observer role. Another center leader was satisfied that preservice teachers were reliable, "caught on real well," and adapted to routines (B.E., interview, 1/5/99). One director, "scrambling to keep his program afloat," felt he "failed" the project by providing too little supervision (C.T., interview, 1/27/99). Two more echoed his concern and wished they had offered more support. In at least two cases, expectations for service learning did not trickle down from agency directors to their staffs. According to one preservice teacher at Head Start, "I started playing with the kids because I didn't know what else to do. The teacher didn't say one word to me. I just didn't know what to do" (S.R., interview, 9/29/98). In contrast, in two contexts where guidance was direct, explicit, and ongoing, preservice teachers moved beyond playing it safe to plan and implement activities and events.

Playing it safe impacted preservice teachers of color in ways similar to their white counterparts. Two preservice teachers appeared to be playing it safer than they actually were. One young woman, described by her community director as "monotone" and "observant," inwardly perceived herself as fully engaged and gaining self-assurance. In a reflective essay she wrote:

> I would never go anywhere without a way back from where I come from. At [church], I went three times without a way back and had no problem getting home. I am not saying I would ask any stranger for a way home, I am expressing how I improved my self-confidence. (N.G., essay, 12/10/98)

Another preservice teacher spent most of her time in a safe tutor role, yet quietly focused her assistance on youth of color at her site. Two other women of color took more strident actions: one accompanied a family to a football game, another participated in an overnight lock-in. In both instances, other factors were at play. The first preservice teacher shared a strong interest in marching band with her young community friend, and the second was prompted to stay overnight by her gregarious, white dorm buddy and classmate.

Most preservice teachers considered themselves increasingly comfortable in their placements. Yet they continued to operate within prescribed service tasks and often overlooked opportunities to reinterpret them from a multicultural perspective. For example, at one community center, preservice teachers developed a reading club. Boyle-Baise encouraged them to construct the initiative around multicultural children's literature. However, the team played it safe and reinforced an ongoing reading incentive program. They encouraged youth to read a quantity of the books on site, regardless of their multicultural potential.

Teacher-Helper

The teacher-helper role dominated service-learning interactions. When asked to assist with a task that was school-related, such as assistance with homework, preservice teachers immediately fell into a teacher role. They offered praise and encouragement, gave hints, and asked questions. As noted earlier, they kept youth on task. Preservice teachers also assumed a teacher-helper role on tasks that were not school-related. For example, when asked to help girls earn a scout badge, one preservice teacher developed a worksheet of questions to assist scouts in learning the necessary background information. The teacher role was easy to assume; after all, this was a field experience for a teacher education course. However, teaching as helping usually was confined to the correct completion of worksheets or textbook assignments. Discussion of youths' personal interests or home lives was carried on primarily outside the teacher-helper role.

Helping kids sometimes was coupled with a "feel-good" rationale. One preservice teacher of color explained it this way: "The first day the kids asked us, 'Can you help me and be my mentor?' I was happy to see that the children were willing to receive all the help they can. Knowing that I was available to work with them made me feel well inside" (C.R., essay, 10/7/98). A white, female preservice teacher told us: "So far, all I thought about is what I'm going to get out of this. Is this going to make me feel good? How can I help other people? Will I be doing good?" (S.J., interview, 9/29/98). This coupling of feeling good, doing good, and helping was reiterated across race and gender lines. For many prospective teachers, helping kids was a major impetus for their service. Through helping, preservice teachers felt important to children's lives, they "made a difference" through assistance as a tutor, mentor, or friend. While viewed as positive by preservice teachers, responses sometimes had missionary tones. Preservice teachers offered something they felt youth lacked—stability, attention, and strong male role models.

For most preservice teachers, across subgroups, service learning was viewed pragmatically, as beneficial to "becoming a better teacher." According to one white, female preservice teacher, "This is a total learning experience for me. I try different things to help kids, just to learn. So, I'll be more comfortable in my classroom" (L.W., interview, 9/29/98). Another preservice teacher eschewed the feel-good rationale for a more practical approach: "I am not at Girl Scouts to feel good about myself or have fun. This experience will prepare me for problems that will arise in my classroom" (S.J., essay, 11/2/98).

Becoming a better teacher had two meanings: understanding more about youth, especially culturally diverse or low-income youngsters; and gaining teaching, especially management, techniques. An example of the first view is the following:

> Their church life is more a main thing than mine. The people at my church didn't come to see me perform because I wasn't their child. It's a family atmosphere there. As a teacher, I need to keep in mind what things are going on different from what I went through. (C.M., interview, 10/19/98)

An example of the second view is this: "I'm learning that kids don't respond to bribery. If you do this, then I'll give you some candy, doesn't work.
I need to be street smarter than the kids to get them to do things" (L.A.,
interview, 10/19/98). The first view was attuned to cultural and community influences on children and teaching. The second view was focused
on control issues, particularly in regard to children of color or from low-
income situations.

Most preservice teachers of color expressed the multicultural position;
they were attentive to cultural and economic differences. However, one
middle-class prospective teacher of color struggled to accept youth from
low-income backgrounds. In reflective essays, she at first denigrated youth
from low-income homes as uninterested in educational experiences and
overly streetwise. In her final essay, she expressed willingness to learn more
about and work with youth from low-income backgrounds. Two other
women of color, from segregated backgrounds, described themselves as
becoming more comfortable and prepared to work in mixed-race situations. The fourth preservice teacher, biracial and comfortable in multicultural situations, utilized service learning to extend her knowledge about
an ethnic group different from her own.

Of the seven white males in the course, four selected church placements (some because the Sunday schedule worked for them). This group
talked and wrote about teaching youth through enthusiasm, compassion,
and parent involvement. They described their experience as "eye-opening,"
particularly about ways in which racism and minority status affected
children's lives. The other three males were placed at community centers
or Head Start. They struggled with deficit notions about youth living in
poverty. Two of the three asserted that youth needed positive male role
models, like themselves. Site placements seemed to matter. Deficit views
were not expressed by males at the churches. There, they witnessed the
presence of supportive families, including affirmative male role models.

Among the thirteen white women, becoming a better teacher had several, shared dimensions. These preservice teachers disrupted stereotypes
and accumulated realistic knowledge about diverse youth. As examples,
preservice teachers recognized that the "perfect vision" of a future classroom
was faulty (M.M., essay, 10/7/98); discovered that deficit notions, especially
about parents, were misleading and wrong (J.F., essay, 11/4/98); learned
not to misjudge the reality kids lived (M.M., essay, 10/20/98); and realized
that youth knew more about "sex, drugs, and violence" than expected (J.K.,
essay, 10/21/98). Learning to handle problematic situations related to difference was repeatedly cited as a useful aspect of service learning.

The teacher-helper role was reinforced by most field situations. Part
of the mutual agreement that underpinned the project was the provision

of quality volunteer service in return for opportunities to learn from the community. Of the six sites, five indicated that the ability to render additional services, however temporary, was a major benefit to them. For most agencies, service centered around tutorial or teacher-aide activities. For example, preservice teachers served as a third person in Head Start classrooms and their volunteer hours were counted as part of the in-kind match for the agency's federal funding. The churches enjoyed extra help with various events, but assistance often broke away from the teacher-helper role.

Regardless of the limits of the teacher-helper role, most community directors agreed with the following assessment: The "experience itself was huge for them. I'm sure that it was" (C.T., interview, 1/27/99). One pastor talked about "bonds" and "friendships" that preservice teachers "may carry with them the rest of their life" (W.M., interview, 2/18/99). Another church leader felt that preservice teachers learned about culture, particularly about the religious influence of the black church upon its children. Although preservice teachers often focused on one-to-one encounters, some translation to the larger picture was expected. For example, at Boys and Girls Club: "Students [preservice teachers] get experience working with kids, large numbers of kids at one time. They work one on one, but they experience 120 kids in here. You know a big group of kids, you know how to handle situations" (B.E., interview, 1/5/99).

For legal and confidence reasons, community directors rarely shared in-depth information about children's backgrounds or pushed relationships beyond teaching and helping. Instead, they cautioned preservice teachers to refer problems back to them. Also, community directors tended to teach indirectly about cultural diversity or poverty. They generally preferred to let the "experience speak for itself" (C.T., interview, 1/27/99). From an atmosphere of welcome and acceptance to messages of God's love across race, to principles of respect and equality, each site practiced high regard for human dignity and equality. Regardless of preservice teachers' immediate activities, directors expected them to "soak up" some of the realities of diversity, poverty, and community via moments of immersion in local life.

Companionship

Service learning offered opportunities to "hang out" with children, something missed in other teacher education classes. According to one preservice teacher: "We learn about teaching everyday, but rarely get to just spend time with kids. Service learning gives us a reason to spend time with kids. That is why we are becoming teachers in the first place!" (S.J., E-mail, 3/5/99). Companionship took time to build and became evident later in the experience. During early visits, preservice teachers actively engaged in activities, such as working at the play-dough table at Head Start. However, interactions were adult-child oriented, one had the power to question or direct the other. Also, conversations tended to turn into teaching-helping situations. As preservice teachers became more comfortable with the situation, companionship evolved.

In the companion role, preservice teachers did activities with students, and conversation was more equal, less forced by the adult, and more casual. Preservice teachers still resorted to the teacher-helper role, but generally, interactions exhibited that of two companions, rather than an adult and child. Companionship was pronounced in settings with older youth, particularly at one community center where preservice teachers spent a lot of time playing pool and video games, watching television, or just talking with youth. Significantly, this rapport had a teacher-oriented end: Preservice teachers sought to gain youth's respect in order to encourage them to participate in a reading club.

As a companion, preservice teachers avoided the assumption of authority. When they needed to counter the wishes of youth, they placed blame on an outside force. For example, in order to quell arguments about the reading quota for earning a free pizza, a preservice teacher responded with, "I don't make the rules" (J.K., field notes, 10/12/98). Further, "I don't make the rules" was an indicator of compliant participation in service learning; often it was something that happened to preservice teachers, rather than being enacted by them.

The time optimally needed to become a companion often exceeded the service-learning cycle. However, increased knowledge of, trust for, and interest in youth and their families was mentioned across all subgroups of preservice teachers. It was illustrated in comments made over time by one white male preservice teacher:

> [Early in the experience] We need to be able to teach kids, not solve their family problems. If I were closer to James and knew his family maybe I could talk to his mother, but I think it is important for me to accept that he has family problems, understand it could affect his learning, and move on. (M.H., essay, 10/7/98)

> [Later in the experience] The kids and I sat down on the steps in the front of the building. They began to question me, to learn who I was. They wanted to see my keys, wallet, and car. They counted my money and told me their dads let them do the same sometimes. At this moment I realized that not every child

at the Club came from a broken home. I wish I could have had
more time to get to know the family background and history of
these kids. (M.H., essay, 11/5/98)

To some extent, companionship was assisted by preservice teachers'
perception that "all kids are just kids." Once the novelty wore off, preservice
teachers begin to see diverse youth as "normal." To most, kids were similar, regardless of ethnic or economic differences. According to one white
male, "The kids at Head Start are mature and independent. Other kids'
moms stay home and do everything for them. Some kids tattle, here they
work it out. For the most part, kids are kids" (G.P., interview, 9/29/98). "Kids
are kids" tended to be articulated by white preservice teachers. This view
shifted the perception of differences from deficits to human universals. While
intended positively, "kids are kids" sometimes glossed over real differences,
such as opportunities related to income. Although similarities and differences, among and within groups of people, were stressed in the multicultural
education course, prospective teachers tended to see commonalities.

A few preservice teachers pricked at the edges of this idea—children
were the same, but . . . for example, one preservice teacher wrote: "Just
when I had decided that all kids were the same, something happened to
change my mind" (S.L., essay, 10/21/98). As this preservice teacher's
change of mind is illustrative, I will share it here in some detail. Continued interactions with a particular 4-year-old at Head Start afforded a
glimpse of difficult life circumstances for this preservice teacher.

A little boy named Larry has caused my change of heart. He is
a 4-year-old filled with more hostility than some people will
know in their lifetime. I have yet to see this little guy smile. On
my way home today, I tried to imagine what his life must be
like. I know his father is not in the picture. His mother just gave
birth to twins. I know his mother isn't too interested in him
because her boyfriend enrolled him in Head Start, and he is
their main contact. (S.L., essay, 10/21/98)

At the time of this writing, the preservice teacher had intervened in a fight
between Larry and another boy. Larry lashed out with fists and foul language. The preservice teacher was asked to hold Larry so he could not hurt
other children. She held him, rocking him as she did her 5-year-old daughter. Larry hugged back. The preservice teacher was unsettled. "At first, I
was furious with him, then I wanted to cry for him. I really worry that
this child will end up in prison." Although the preservice teacher once

thought the world's problems could be solved by giving children love and attention, she now recognized further assistance was needed for Larry.

This critical incident became a focal point of a reflective class session. As mentioned earlier, quotations from preservice teacher's reflective essays were used to prompt discussion. In this case, Boyle-Baise selected a quote from another part of the preservice teacher's writings about Larry:

> My community experience is opening my eyes to the fact that the majority of children do not live in a perfect world. I now realize that a child's behavior can be the result of many factors. I have to look for reasons for the behavior, not just stop the behavior. My blinders have kept me from realizing that even in our town kids are hungry, abused, scared, or lonely." (S.L., essay, 10/21/98)

Although the quotation was presented anonymously, the preservice teacher volunteered to tell her story. Boyle-Baise then urged the class to contemplate what social or economic factors their "blinders" keep them from seeing. Responses were tinged with stereotypes. Preservice teachers knew little about the real circumstances of children's home lives. Boyle-Baise also responded to this situation from afar. A response to this dilemma, shared control for multicultural service learning with community partners, is described in Chapter 5.

Preservice teachers who grappled with dualistic notions of youth's lives—"kids are kids, but . . ."—were a select group. Several preservice teachers of color, one white, nontraditional student (and mother), another white preservice teacher from California, and one white male who had attended Montessori schools brought forth these concerns. Prior life experience, especially with diversity, seemed to influence this perception.

Companionship depended, at least in part, on time, and time was too short. Every community director identified time constraints as the low point of the course. According to the parent coordinator at Head Start: "They just get to know the kids, and kids get to know them, and they leave" (N.M., interview, 2/9/99). One director worried that preservice teachers left with just a glimpse of the context. Another pastor was concerned that bonds were temporary and unreal:

> I get disappointed when I see that if our children pick up a bond, it's a temporary one, real at the time, but not for real. . . . When they see another set of students [preservice teachers] come in they might get the attitude—I don't want anything to do with them. (B.H., interview, 1/26/99)

Some directors suggested an extension of service-learning projects to the next semester in order to offer longer term relationships.

These three roles and perspectives do not constitute a continuum, from playing it safe to teacher-helper, to companion. Preservice teachers commonly operated within approved, safe roles. This approach is sensible for short-term visitors to another's world. They usually functioned as teacher/helpers, but often this task was prescribed for them. In contrast, one preservice teacher of color was remembered by her community director as always holding a baby or young child, at ease, willing to tackle any task. She gave and received companionship from the moment she walked in the door. Yet, there does seem to be a progression toward companionship as a function of contact and time. Companionship had the most potential for the course aim of learning more about youth and families, but general experience in the thick of a diverse context was fruitful for multicultural education as well.

EXPERIENCE SPEAKS FOR ITSELF

What really happens in community service learning experiences? What do preservice teachers do that supports or limits reconsideration of their Eurocentric views? Do certain experiences spur self-examination and realization? Are there constraints to the learning process? Can experiences be altered to generate cultural insights and motivate social critique?

In this case, what really happened was learning through service, mostly in prescribed roles, in affirmative, culturally diverse situations. Preservice teachers focused on youth, primarily as teachers and helpers for them. This constrained their knowledge of adults, families, and community resources, but opened their eyes to cultural norms and life situations for youth. They received some instruction and guidance from community liaisons—enough to function in the context, but rarely enough to fully understand it. Nevertheless, the experience spoke for itself. Preservice teachers were immersed, at least momentarily, in neighborhoods from which many of their future students will come. There was quality to "being there." Preservice teachers had opportunities to interact cross-culturally, disrupt stereotypes, experience community resourcefulness, and learn to work positively with diverse youth.

Preservice teachers certainly could have gone beyond the roles and perspectives described. A major challenge is to rethink such projects in ways that support more assertive engagement from preservice teachers and offer them deeper connections with youth, families, and communities. The factors that strongly influenced the field experience serve as a starting place for this reconsideration.

Sites

If experience speaks for itself, then community service learning sites matter a great deal. Here, service-learning sites were located in a low-income neighborhood of a small, fairly affluent college town. Outside the university, the population of color was small. The church sites included many African American members, and congregations varied in education and income levels. The low-income neighborhood was modest and acute conditions of poverty (as indicated by subsidized housing) were limited. As a result, preservice teachers interacted with a wide range of people of color and with whites from low income situations. For these preservice teachers, many from small- or middle-size in-state homogeneous towns, interactions with these groups offered powerful, novel experiences with diversity. The biographies of preservice teachers impact what is novel, or outside their prior life experience. This point is considered in another section below.

In order to reinforce the major messages of the multicultural education course, it is fundamental that what happens inside service-learning sites affirms cultural diversity, challenges inequity, and supports educational equality and excellence. Each organization did so, but in ways that opened different doors for preservice teachers. In the churches, preservice teachers were able to interact with entire families. Preservice teachers placed there expressed positive views of parents and families. In community centers, where preservice teachers primarily worked one-on-one with youth, they articulated more information about children, especially about teaching techniques responsive to diversity. A mix of these knowledge bases is necessary to achieve the aims of multicultural education. Site locations should be potentially rich in contacts with youth and parents and willing to involve preservice teachers in situations oriented to families.

Tasks

While the teacher-helper role had its place and companionship was desirable, by themselves these roles played it too safe for multicultural education. Preservice teachers often perceived children as learners, much as they would in a school-based field experience. A primary reason for service learning beyond school boundaries is to learn to situate children as family and community members and to view both as sources of knowledge about and strength for youth. Interactions with families and instruction about community issues occurred here, but it was spotty. An expansion and diversification of educative tasks, across all learning sites, could strengthen service learning as a field experience for multicultural education. For example, attendance at community events, such as evening reading circles and parent meetings at Head Start, offered contact with adults and motivated reconsideration of stereotypes, particularly of perceptions of parents as uncaring or uninvolved in their children's lives. The development of an event, such as the Hallelujah party, opened doors to acquaintanceship with a wide range of community people. The completion of mini-inquiries or Why?-Studies, which required in-group (insider) and out-group (library) sources, engaged preservice teachers in conversations with site directors and other adults and youth within agencies. The iteration of such tasks as required dimensions of service learning could move preservice teachers beyond one-on-one tutoring roles. The completion of an array of tasks could offer more insight into diverse or low-income communities.

Community Contact Person

Community directors were selected primarily for their potential to serve as cultural brokers to the local community. Either the person was a member of the group served, or had grown up in the neighborhood, or had worked effectively in the locale for a long while. The promise of community connection was realized partially. The directors were dissatisfied with their guidance and supervision of preservice teachers and wanted to do more. To some extent, they were crippled by other, heavy demands on their time, but this will always be the case. How can educators tap into the potential of community brokers? The framework set for service learning (at the orientation lunch) was insufficient to motivate vigorous involvement from community directors. Given the willingness of directors to do more, a specific list of community service-learning activities that supplement multicultural education might motivate and guide their leadership. Movement toward stronger partnership, possibly the designation of directors as coteachers, might also spur their interest and commitment. For example, in the development of a variety of field-based tasks, community representatives should play a collaborative role.

Biography

The major "punch" or power of this community service learning experience was exposure to people and settings significant to preservice teacher's future classrooms, yet outside their previous life experiences.

Service learning jolted most preservice teachers from assumed (often biased) views of culturally diverse youth, of poverty, and of teaching in pluralistic situations. Because prospective teachers came from varied backgrounds, the service-learning experience spoke differently to each person. For many white teacher candidates, service learning in culturally diverse contexts was a first intensive interaction with people of color. For many preservice teachers with enough affluence to attend a major university, service learning was a real confrontation with youth in poverty. For preservice teachers of color who grew up in segregated, minority communities, service learning offered extended experience in multiracial situations. The biography of preservice teachers matters. Service learning is a developmental endeavor related to previous life experience. If service learning is to foster heightened awareness of culture, race, and power, then situations and activities must be carefully considered in terms of their power to offer new insights. Advance knowledge of preservice teachers' backgrounds is key, particularly to structure potentially powerful learning experiences for them.

Course Instructor

Boyle-Baise was committed to community service learning; in her mind, multicultural education without a community touchstone was abstract and shallow. She carefully structured the course and the field experience to build upon each other. She taught the course and monitored the field experience. However, oversight for service learning was a teaching overload and her time could not stretch to offer much presence in the field. Given the real constraints of field roles and activities, some of the inward struggles of students about their biases must be attributed primarily to the multicultural education course.

Once the service-learning framework was in place, field activities were left to the discretion of community directors. This stance relinquished control of the field experience and stymied some course aims. A messier, more hands-on, continually collaborative orientation to community connections is needed in order to meet university and community aims and needs.

THE PROMISE OF COMMUNITY SERVICE LEARNING

What really happened did not realize fully the promise of community service learning for multicultural education. Preservice teachers reported a great deal of self-growth. They bonded with new friends across cultural and economic lines; they grappled with their own biases; and they gained responsive teaching strategies. Yet, preservice teachers' links to and understandings of family and community strengths and problems were weak. Some shortcomings can reasonably be resolved through reconfiguration of the service-learning project. Several proposals for impacting influential factors were discussed here.

In the next chapter, community service learning is reconfigured to more closely match the vision of multicultural service learning outlined in Chapter 2. Knowledge about what really happened and about what preservice teachers thought about it spurred a reconstruction of experience to more intensively underscore multicultural education and connect to communities. As I will show, the key to both lay in sharing control of service learning with community liaisons and, in so doing, constructing robust community partnerships from more superficial university-community associations.

Looking Back, Planning Forward: Lynne's Reflections

Multicultural service learning had not lived up to its promise. Still, enough good had come from my previous round of service learning, that I was not ready to throw in the towel. As I looked back on what really happened within community service learning, I knew that reconstruction of the effort was necessary. I wondered how to keep the most promising and set aside the most problematic aspects of the experience.

It was problematic for preservice teachers to merely "fit in" to prescribed volunteer roles, usually centered around one-on-one remedial teaching assistance. In so doing, they missed more casual, friendly contacts that could acquaint them with kids as cultural beings and as community members. Adults and families stood at the fringes of service learning instead of at its center as resources for teaching. Directors of local organizations offered insufficient guidance, leaving their potential leadership untapped. I had my hands full in teaching the multicultural education course, which left service learning too loosely supervised. On the other hand, preservice teachers from diverse backgrounds became more comfortable with youth and adults different from themselves. They practiced teaching a range of youth like their future students. They came to know some families, especially at church sites. And many undertook serious self-assessment about teaching diverse and low-income youth.

When I looked back and planned forward, I realized two things: (1) I needed more help to make service a vital, provocative learning experience; and (2) I needed to develop learning tasks that fostered interaction with youth and families, outside tutoring roles. It was easy to see that help was at hand; my community associates could assume more responsibility to mentor preservice teachers placed in their organizations. Few enjoy taking responsibility for someone else's program; my associates and I would have to rebuild the service-learning project together.

CHAPTER 5

The Spirit of Shared Control

MARILYNNE BOYLE-BAISE with JONI CLARK,
BART EPLER, WILLIAM McCOY, GWEN PAULK,
NANCY SLOUGH, and CHRIS TRUELOCK

This chapter and the next represent a major shift in my approach to multicultural service learning, the result of lessons learned from my experience with service learning. I recognized the more problematic and promising aspects of multicultural service learning. In response, I moved from association with community representatives to partnership, from casual field supervision to contractual instruction, and from tangential contact with parents to required interaction among families. The spirit of shared control epitomized this partnership; it stood for interdependence, mutual respect, and collective endeavor. In this chapter, the essence of this spirit is taken apart in order to afford an inside view of our partnership. In the next chapter, the practice or exercise of shared control is described. The two chapters should be read in tandem as *thinking* about and *doing* multicultural service learning in coalition with culturally diverse, local community leaders. In recognition of our partnership, this chapter is coauthored with my community liaisons, and written in terms of the collective *we*.

Voices and views of the community are rare to investigations of service learning. Cruz and Giles (2000) find such a void in the literature that they wonder, "Where's the community in service-learning research?" They suppose that community is a knotty domain of study. It is difficult to define, confounding in complexity, and demanding for practitioners. Cruz and Giles pose a four-pronged approach for the study of community: (1) The university-community partnership should be the unit of analysis; (2) the partnership should demonstrate good service-learning principles; (3) action research should be the preferred methodology; and (4) inquiry should focus on assets in the community. This approach supposedly avoids fruitless arguments over the nature of community and allows generalization across studies. It puts the principles of service learning to work and permits their examination. It advocates research with community partners and, in so doing, honors commitment to them. Finally, it emphasizes what is present in communities, the capacities of its residents and associations, rather than what is absent, the problems or needs of its neighborhood (Kretzman & McKnight, 1993).

Our efforts to share control, though initiated prior to this call, reso-nate with this model. We focused on ourselves, on our partnership, based on cooperative, experiential inquiry, a form of action research (Reason, 1994). The spirit of shared control stands for our commitment to reciprocal, mutually beneficial, jointly enacted community service and learning. A major aim was to acquaint preservice teachers with assets in communi-ties, no matter how marginalized or economically distressed. Most of us, as leaders for local community churches and social organizations, embody these assets. In this chapter, we selectively cull from two research forums, occasions when we came together to reflect on our partnership and on our development of a multicultural service-learning project.

WHERE'S THE COMMUNITY IN
SERVICE-LEARNING RESEARCH?

Studies of community participation in service learning are few and far between. However, several inquiries offer findings pertinent to our partnership and to the spirit of shared control. We describe them briefly here, then return to them later, as reference points for our work.

B. A. Miller (1997) found that consensual, common visions for com-munity development united rural communities and spurred local action. Partnerships were strengthened though collaborative project development and by leadership from students, teachers, and community people. Leader-ship was defined as a shared responsibility, rather than the right of a few elected or hired individuals. A project coordinator, who sustained the involvement of key stakeholders over time, was vital to the project.

Gelmon and colleagues (1998) investigated community perceptions of service learning as part of field training for health professions. As in the Miller study, partnerships were strengthened by a strong sense of engagement, reciprocity, and mutuality. Involvement of community representatives in campus roles, especially as coteachers, direct relationships with faculty, and ongoing communication fostered engagement. University responsiveness to community concerns, especially to overstretched service capacities, and recognition of communities as knowledge sources heightened reciprocity.

Community organizations benefited from increased understanding of their missions and from networking with other agencies. Also, due to volunteer assistance, service levels temporarily increased. Partnerships were organic, heavily dependent upon the particular people involved.

Vernon and Ward (1999) surveyed 65 directors of community service agencies who worked with colleges or universities on service learning projects. Similar to Gelmon's study, they found that service learning was perceived positively, as a way to meet agency goals and to fill program gaps. Agency directors wanted increased communication with colleges; they needed a grasp of course goals for service learning and of their responsibilities in achievement of them. Directors asked to be coteachers, a role that fostered reciprocity in the Gelmon study.

B. A. Miller (1997) noted that community development faltered when collaborative relationships among diverse cultural and political groups, such as ranchers, town dwellers, environmentalists, and Hispanics, could not be built. Also, tensions between teachers and communities (stemming from school-bond defeats) stymied community building. Except for this reference, issues related to race, culture, and power are overlooked in community studies. The vitality of common visions, mutual interests, joint leadership, and coteaching, emphasized in these studies, resonate with community-building orientations to multicultural service learning (outlined in Chapter 2).

The following questions about a university-community partnership are addressed below: What did partnership mean to community participants in a multicultural service-learning project? What did shared control mean to community participants in a multicultural service-learning project? Responses are related to and inform the research outlined above.

THE PROJECT

Multicultural service learning was a one-credit-hour field experience linked to a three-credit-hour multicultural education course. Preservice teachers offered 20 hours of their time and service to churches and community organizations in a culturally diverse, low-income area of a small, university town. These organizations primarily targeted the immediate geographic neighborhood, but also reached out to people in the whole town. Lynne Boyle-Baise considered them good placements for a field experience for multicultural education: Views of clientele were affirmative; leadership included people from the groups served; activities offered positive, cross-group interaction; and membership included youth and families. Typically, teams of four or five preservice teachers served at each site.

Boyle-Baise taught the multicultural education course and facilitated its service-learning dimension. The rest of us were leaders in the organizations served. We were a mixed group of African American and European American men and women, from varied cultural and occupational backgrounds. Our partnership included two pastors, one for a racially mixed congregation, the other for a predominately black church; a director of a university program for students of color and education director for the black church; the program director for Boys and Girls Club; the director of a community center; the parent coordinator for Head Start; and a teacher education professor.

At the time of this project, Boyle-Baise valued service learning as a feasible, responsible framework for interactions with culturally diverse and low-income communities. Yet, she was dissatisfied with her prior service-learning efforts. Our diverse group collaborated to reconstruct multicultural service learning, from the inside-out and bottom-up. We developed a task-based contract to guide preservice teachers in the field. We served as coteachers for service learning: participating in a service-learning orientation; leading discussion during reflective class sessions; reading and reviewing preservice teachers' reflective essays, and evaluating preservice teachers' work in the field. We also supervised the service-learning field experience. (See Chapter 6 for examples of these dimensions of our work.)

THE INQUIRY

Lynne Boyle-Baise was intrigued by cooperative, experiential inquiry groups, as defined by Reason and Heron (1986) and Reason (1994). In this orientation to inquiry, a group studies itself. Members of the group become coresearchers whose perspectives contribute to the project and cosubjects who participate in the activity under investigation. The inquiry centers around interchange of ideas, decision making, and joint planning. This stance resonated with a spirit of shared control for service learning. It afforded expression of diverse views, and it honored the cooperative intent of our partnership.

We created a cooperative, experiential inquiry group. We shared our beliefs, values, and views. Boyle-Baise was a full member of the inquiry group, a facilitator at best. The differences among us served the role of devil's advocate, an internal check on our perceptions and suggestions. Over the summer, prior to the fall course, we met three times, for several hours each time, to discuss, reconsider, and ultimately transform multicultural service learning. Then we met for reflective conversations three times during the fall semester: at the outset of service learning, at midterm, and at semester's end. On these occasions, we reflected upon our partnership and upon our efforts to share control.

Early on, we searched for a way to articulate our positions that allowed each voice and version to be heard. We opted to write as a team, rather than to depict our experience through Boyle-Baise's voice as sole author. We decided to highlight two of our reflective conversations (on September 8 and December 10, 1999). We thought of these occasions as research forums. We responded to a roster of questions that framed, but did not wholly set our conversation (see Appendix B for the question sets). In the following section, quotations from transcripts of the forums highlight key points about community partnership and shared control. The chapter was reviewed, modified, and accepted by the partnership that we became.

PARTNERSHIPS AND SHARED CONTROL

What did *partnership* mean to community participants in a multi-cultural service-learning project? The interpretation of partnership centered around three interrelated and overlapping notions: reciprocity, mutuality, and power.[1]

Partnership as Reciprocity

Partnership meant reciprocity; benefits were perceived by both sides. Teacher education gained a culturally diverse, authentic community context for teacher preparation. Community organizations gained responsible temporary assistance and participation in teacher training. Reciprocity was a 50-50 arrangement, which met aims and needs of both parties. A sense of equivalence is articulated in several reasons for participation in the project. Bart Epler expressed his reason as follows:

> From hearing about the project, I decided it would be good for us and our agency and for the students. They can see how kids interact, emotionally what sets them off, what they can do to help them, to keep them going and focused. For me it's a 50-50 thing, great for us and them. (9/8/99)

Reasoning along similar lines, Chris Truelock pointed out, "It's a good experience for everybody. The students are exposed to situations they

---

1. In quoted material, *students* refers to preservice teachers, unless otherwise indicated.

might not see otherwise. Its neat for me to see students fresh and new and learn from them. It is a good evaluation process for me to see what they write in their journals" (9/8/99). From Reverend W. McCoy's perspective, "To commune means to go out of your comfort zone and communicate. As a church, it's the best thing for us to do. As part of a service-learning program, we can help students understand that we all share the same humanity. It's creating ties that bind" (9/8/99).

Reciprocity defined the interrelationship between teaching and learning in the university and in the community. Future teachers were situated inside the community to meet youth and families and to identify local resources for teaching. Community representatives were invited inside the university to assist in the preparation of teachers for the neighborhood children. The following quotes illustrate benefits for preservice teachers and for community partners. According to Gwen Paulk,

> Partnership serves two purposes. One, for students to better understand families, how they connect with the education of their own children and how a child is not just what they see in the classroom. There are a lot of influences of families and church. Two, it was good for our church because we developed a tutoring program. (12/10/99)

Bart Epler found that participation in the project sparked his own learning:

> It was, to me, a great learning tool for students who are going to be teaching. I was able to give my expertise to them and learn from them. It was a motivation thing, it sparked it back in me. Because they wanted to find out information, I learned not to take things for granted, not just make assumptions. (12/10/99)

Reciprocity meant balanced interchange, a sense of being fully vested in the project and commensurate with one another. It was not appropriate for Lynne Boyle-Baise to place preservice teachers in the community and hope for the best, nor was it proper for us to use them as good volunteer help, then let them go. Both parties were equal participants in a quality multicultural service-learning experience. For Chris Truelock, this meant an increased commitment to service learning:

> I've seen different ways we deal with students. Failures come when there is no interaction between the students and the staff. It was important for my commitment that this year I, and my

staff, offered students what they needed. It's not healthy for students to come without opportunities for guidance and reflection. (9/8/99)

Opportunities for networking among community leaders was an unexpected bonus of our exchange. As a result of our discussions about service learning, we learned from each other and initiated collegial relationships. Relationship building underpinned the partnership, but, as Kretzmann and McKnight (1993) note, it also fostered a sense of interdependence within the neighborhood itself. According to Nancy Slough, "This project established relationships with other agencies in the community. I wasn't sure what went on at Boys and Girls Club, now I know Bart. I have a contact person there, and he has me here" (12/10/99).

Reciprocal relations were not without issue. A major obstacle was the brief tenure of preservice teachers in the community; activities initiated and relationships kindled suddenly halted at semester's end. Our town was dominated by the university and accustomed to semester schedules, albeit not always happily. Time constraints tarnished the serious business of making friends and cultivating colleagues. Several partners discussed time constraints with their teams, from continuing projects they initiated to informing children and parents about the end of their service. For example, Gwen Paulk recalled the following conversation:

I met with my team last night. We talked about our visions for their help. We discussed tutoring. They can really benefit kids in our church. It is not something our church has done before. We talked about the drawbacks, like what will happen when they are gone. The church will have to take over. The service learning experience is too short. When it is over, then what? (9/8/99)

Partnership as Mutuality

Partnership meant mutuality; a sense of common vision, shared venture, and conjoint endeavor. Mutuality stemmed from intensive conversations about goals for service *and* learning as part of multicultural teacher education (see Chapter 6 for detailed plans of this project). We envisioned a service learning where youth and families were affirmed, regardless of their cultural group identity or economic status. We recognized service learning as an occasion to meet people different from oneself, and we planned for positive, sustained interactions between preservice teachers and members of our organizations. We stood ready to address tough issues that arose daily, in order to help preservice teachers wrestle with realities of anger, hate, or unfairness. Chris Truelock expressed our sense of shared obligation to these aims in this way:

> I and my organization have an obligation to help future educators understand hard-to-reach populations. . . . I want students to realize that when the school day is over the student's day does not end. Our day starts where school leaves off. We all need to realize that it takes a village to raise a child. (9/8/99)

Mutuality opened the door to team teaching and to joint inquiry. Lynne Boyle-Baise no longer needed to assume sole leadership, either as teacher or researcher. Each partner had special expertise to offer prospective teachers and singular views to present for research. The idea of coteaching and coresearching took on credence. Mutuality built community. As Reverend McCoy described, it fostered the feeling that "we're part of something. We have more heart and soul in it—all of us" (9/8/99). We jointly contributed to something worthwhile.

Partnership as Power

Partnership meant power; community-based learning and community people as teacher educators were validated. Community-based service learning was emphasized as central to the multicultural education course, not just fluff. Power accrued from extensive involvement in the entire service-learning experience. Community instructors felt taken seriously, and they took themselves and the project seriously as well. As Gwen Paulk noted, "The reflection papers gave us a chance to . . . give our comments. Students did not feel they were doing a fluff activity. We took part in grading and that gave our comments validity. . . . I felt students valued what we said" (12/10/99).

Power was also personal, an empowerment, or moment of growth. Participation jostled some of us from the rut of routine, helped us work more effectively with volunteers, or fostered our self-confidence. According to Gwen Paulk, "This project is developing me. It is helping me have more confidence in what I say and how I present it. I've enjoyed being in on planning this project" (9/8/99). Reverend McCoy described his participation as a joyful extension of his church work: "This program is tailor-made for me. It fits the message of our church. I get joy out of seeing a program on campus that fosters the same ideas as our church. It is a spiral for me" (12/10/99).

Another noteworthy aspect of empowerment, not expressed in the forums, but tacitly acknowledged, was the power of legitimacy for Boyle-

Baise and for the multicultural education course. The course, and her instruction, garnered respect from its ground in an authentic, culturally diverse, community context. This valuation was significant for Boyle-Baise, as a white multicultural educator. Our community partnership offered her (and preservice teachers) the power of access to constituent groups for multicultural education, especially to youth of color or from low-income households and their families.

What did *shared control* mean to community participants in a multicultural service-learning project? Shared control was a guide or watchword for reciprocity, mutuality, and power. It actualized all three. Shared control was setting the criteria for top-notch, multicultural service learning and "seeing what happened" (W.M., 12/10/99). It was "an opportunity to review reflective essays, grade the service learning, and give feedback about the service dimension of the course" (N.S., 9/8/99). Shared control countered a sense of being objectified, as part of an experimental venture into community, often felt by local recipients of volunteer service. Gwen Paulk expressed this change in tone in the following way:

> Shared control, it takes us out of the guinea pig role to actually becoming educators. Now, I have the responsibility to help guide young people, to point out things they might overlook. I am responsible to help them understand what it means to be a multicultural person, not a passive bystander. (9/8/l99)

Meanings for Shared Control

For all partners, shared control spurred thoughts of evaluation. The idea of *control* was connected to the service-learning grade. When asked to consider the most problematic or promising aspect of shared control, partners jointly exclaimed: "Grading!" Shared control offered the clout of judgement, but carried its responsibility as well. According to Reverend J. Clark, it was a task not to be taken lightly: "We [preservice teachers and community partner] discuss how we can work together. We participate in their grade. That's scary, it is more responsibility. We have to pay close, close attention to where students are when they come in and when they end up" (9/8/99).

Chris Truelock grappled with nomenclature. He thought the term *shared control* generated a sense of harshness. He preferred to think of our partnership as a shared experience. "I think *control* is a harsh word. I look at it as a shared experience for everybody. It's a shared experience for the students and for us" (9/8/99).

For most partners, shared control stood for joint responsibility for the entire service-learning project. Reverend McCoy put it this way: "All of the responsibility for the program does not fall on anyone's part. It is dispersed between us, even the grading. We can make changes. It all helps the program" (9/8/99). As witness to shared control, partners freely suggested improvements for service learning. They proposed the creation of a video in which preservice teachers would introduce their placement sites to a subsequent group of service learners and the modification of grading criteria to include aspects of personal responsibility and initiative.

Dimensions of Shared Control

The role of coteacher underscored shared control. It recognized and legitimated community people and local knowledge. An unexpected bonus of shared control was partners' feedback on preservice teachers' reflective essays. This form of response developed spontaneously from our summer meetings. During one meeting, a partner proposed the idea as a way to tap and respond to preservice teachers' views related to service learning. The rest of us quickly agreed to tackle the reviews. Lynne Boyle-Baise saw this as a novel approach to coinstruction and as another venue for our voices and views to be heard.

The review of reflective essays met our highest expectations. It deepened our insights into preservice teachers' assumptions and biases. It afforded an occasion to debunk stereotypes and to discuss culture and race. Gwen Paulk appreciated this opportunity: "I really liked being able to read the papers and give feedback. There were so many stereotypes in the beginning papers. I was able to explain what was not acceptable" (12/10/99). Chris Truelock emphasized the value of feedback from people on-site, close to the service-learning experience. He noted that "the comments made were points only people on-site could make" (12/10/99). He argued that while Boyle-Baise might catch a lot of general stereotypes, community partners could challenge deficit views of local situations. As noted in Chapter 4, issues raised in essays often became the basis for reflective class discussions. According to Reverend McCoy, "It really let us know where they are, what they learned. . . . One student asked me, how can I become a more multicultural educator. That is the whole point of this project!" (12/10/99).

The task-based contract structured shared control. The tasks matched aims for multicultural education with needs and activities of community organizations. For example, learning about youth and families was a key goal for multicultural service learning. In order to glimpse "funds of knowledge" (Moll, Amanti, Neff, & Gonzalez, 1992), or specialized information or talent found within families, preservice teachers were asked to interact with one family in depth. Options for this task included shadowing a family for a day, sharing a meal or attending a family event, or observing on a home visit. According to Bart Epler, the tasks were realistic, "legit," or "things that can be done" (12/10/99). Chris Truelock used the contract as a guideline or blueprint. The contract helped both him and his service-learning team organize and monitor their field experience. Truelock noticed that "students brought it out and checked where they were at" (12/10/99). Reverend McCoy echoed this position: The task-based contract "kept us on our toes" as a framework and time line for multicultural service learning (12/10/99). Additionally, Gwen Paulk thought that utilization of the task-based contract "helped solidify the partnership" (12/10/99). We built solidarity through our development, use, and support of the contract. It was an authentic artifact of collective endeavor.

We submitted service-learning grades for individuals on our site teams, and our role in evaluation accented our shared control. We discussed our evaluations with Lynne Boyle-Baise, who retained final responsibility for service-learning grades. Invariably, she upheld our judgments. In one case, a preservice teacher questioned her grade. Then, one of the partners and Boyle-Baise convened a three-way conference and responded to the preservice teacher's concerns.

Completion of the contract and of 20 hours in the field, and demonstration of team leadership originally seemed to be sound criteria for letter grades (i.e., A, B, or C), but, as Reverend McCoy pointed out, problems with attendance did not "fit on this sheet" (12/10/99). (For original evaluation criteria, see Appendix C.) Our benchmarks overlooked meaningful measures of social engagement, such as reliability and responsibility. Chris Truelock "almost pulled out a standard staff evaluation form, but we didn't agree on that from the beginning. So, I graded them on: did they do tasks, did they show up on time, were they caring about service?" (12/10/99). Nancy Slough compared our standards with criteria for staff evaluations at Head Start. She suggested that in order to improve the contract, "we need some criteria that show growth, like our staff evaluation. We could include: initiative, creativity, responsibility, and dependability" (12/10/99).

Demands of Shared Control

Shared control for teaching and learning was demanding for all parties. We stayed in touch through meetings before, during, and after the period of service learning. We read three sets of reflective essays. We ensured that at least two partners attended and directed reflective class sessions. We supervised preservice teachers and arranged for completion of their contract tasks. Was it too much of a good thing? We differed in our responses to this question. Some of us found our level of participation "enough," or "just right," and for others it was "too much." We found our contribution rewarding, but meetings of all sorts—planning, orienting preservice teachers, leading class discussions, checking goals at midterm, debriefing after the project—cut into our hectic schedules. Except for reductions in meetings, however, the project and the partnership withstood our initial efforts. We remained close-knit and proud of our initiative. The following quotes represent the range of our views. According to Nancy Slough,

> In order to have a true partnership, I think you have to expect this level of participation. For me, I simply do not have the time to spare. My schedule is very hectic, I work evening hours, I am in and out of the building a lot. Next time, I could share my responsibilities with a partner in our organization. I need to make some changes internally in order to participate, but not in the project per se. (12/10/99)

For Chris Truelock, the project compounded an increased work load. Yet, he was gratified by his level of commitment to service learning:

> My center has never seen more activities. But, last year I wasn't happy with what I gave to the project. So, I made the decision to do more. For the most part, it was just right. I enjoyed getting out of this building, it was nice to listen to a college class. It was a good wholesome experience. (12/10/99)

Bart Epler struggled with so many meetings, but recognized their worth to the project. "Maybe it was a little too much participation. We met a lot. You could try to cut out some meetings somewhere. On the other hand, the meetings are necessary. They helped us build the program" (12/10/99).

Lynne Boyle-Baise nurtured our partnership through attention to details. During the summer, several of us ran youth camps and missed monthly meetings. After each meeting, we received a note and copy of the agenda. Chris Truelock recalled, "It was hard for me to meet in the summer. As far as the planning process, I felt very good about it. I appreciated the several calls and letters sent to me. I felt the process was well organized" (9/8/99). Additionally, the pastor of one church was transferred. The newly appointed pastor, Joni Clark, agreed to continue the church's involvement in service learning. She expressed her approval: "When I met with Lynne and Gwen, they had a packet and brought me up to speed. I think it says something about a project when you can bring a newcomer

in" (9/8/99). Bart Epler found the "memos and calling are really important" to keeping our group together. "All the other stuff I'm working on
fizzles" (12/10/99). Constant attention to details of communication helped
ensure that our project did not fizzle.

PUTTING COMMUNITY INTO
SERVICE-LEARNING RESEARCH

Our project illustrates the approach proposed by Cruz and Giles (2000).
It focuses on the community partnership as the unit of analysis, demonstrates good service-learning principles, utilizes action research as a method
of self-study, and involves local leaders as assets for the community. Each
of these points is considered in turn.

Four-Point Approach

A partnership focus is not a community focus. To view the community through the lens of the partnership is to see it secondhand. The study
of our partnership reveals its internal workings, rather than its external
influences. Our partnership drew from a geographic and cultural community; it represented some of the community's leadership. Daily concerns
of organizations, such as insufficient personnel and funding cuts, impacted
our partnership, especially in the form of increased demands on the time
and energy of our members. Also, neighborhood issues, particularly those
that involved youth, surfaced during reflective discussions (see Chapter 6
for examples). However, the character of the community, as it exists outside service-learning sites, remains in the background.

A partnership focus offers, instead, a snapshot of community building. In this case, the partnership crossed professional, geographic, cultural,
and economic lines. It coalesced around the idea of shared control.

Our partnership was a living example of conjoint endeavor. We exemplified the interdependency that characterizes quality service and learning. We acted as a team, being there as a presence in the classroom and in
the community. Our roles as codevelopers, coteachers, and coresearchers
placed us in interwoven capacities. To our mutual benefit, community
learning was accentuated, cross-group relations were kindled, and teacher
preparation was shared. The power of instruction and evaluation was dispersed, which empowered community partners and validated the multicultural education course.

Service-learning principles of reciprocity and mutuality took on added
meaning as part of a multicultural education course. Reciprocity stood for

the development of an equal, affirmative, culturally diverse coalition. Mutuality involved the preparation of teachers of credit to the university and of promise for culturally diverse or low-income youth.

Cooperative experimental inquiry, or action research, worked for us for several reasons. In method, it centered inquiry on service learning. This focus left most of our work and personal lives alone. We considered this limitation appropriate. There was little cause for inquiry into our lives, beyond the immediate project. Personal challenges and changes impacted our capacity for participation. For example, one of us grappled with a new job and another of us married during the service-learning project. Although these events had little outward influence on the project, they heightened hardships of involvement. A limited focus on service-learning offered assurances that inquiry would remain a bounded, professional endeavor.

The tone of cooperative inquiry matched our sense of collective effort. The parity of partnership, as coteachers and coresearchers, also affirmed cultural diversity and social equality—fundamental aims for multicultural education. Moreover, ongoing dialogue afforded opportunities to assess the project as it went along.

Shared control demonstrated an asset or capacity-driven model. It legitimated the community as a people, place, and thing invaluable for multicultural teacher education. It identified community leaders as local assets. It prepared prospective teachers to search for such assets in order to gain understanding and build linkages supportive of their future students. It allowed the community to invest in future teachers for children like their own. It was "relationship-driven" (Kretzmann & McKnight, 1993, p. 9) in that it built community, particularly among the seven partners, but also between the university and community, and between members of community associations and the preservice teachers they hosted.

Relation to Other Studies

The spirit and function of our partnership reinforces and extends findings from other community studies (Gelmon et al., 1998; B. A. Miller, 1997; Vernon & Ward, 1999). Similar to the Miller and Gelmon studies, a strong sense of common endeavor, nurtured through collaborative project development and implementation, sustained our university-community partnership. Distinct from these studies, our partnership cultivated cross-cultural collaboration. Our association was not new, rather it underwent a metamorphosis from university dominion to shared control. At the outset, a degree of trust existed, enough to question our previous approach. Although what really happened in prior cycles of service learning "played it too safe" for multicultural education (as reported in Chapter 4), community connections had been initiated. Possibly, shared control is a second-stage process, or at least an endeavor dependent upon a foundation of acquaintance and respect.

The dispersion of leadership solidified the partnership and empowered the partners. As Lynne Boyle-Baise relinquished control for instruction, we picked it up. Joint leadership necessitated a relocation of power. As part of the disruption of status quo relations of power, the university representative was not the lone researcher. Instead, we became core-searchers and tackled the task of self-study.

Unlike findings from Vernon and Ward, our mutual benefits extended beyond "filling gaps" in programs. A primary mission for this endeavor was movement beyond volunteer work to learning about and from communities. Service learners fulfilled a task-based contract that included service to organizations and opportunities to learn from them.

As noted in all previous studies, ongoing communication was key to a successful partnership. As observed by B. A. Miller and Gelmon, our collective benefitted from active involvement of a faculty member. Her engagement was quite demanding; it stretched her capacities similarly to the rigors of our participation. Different from earlier studies, our partnership was almost overwhelmed by ongoing meetings and activities. Multiple meetings to develop, operate, and evaluate multicultural service learning, pushed partners to the limits of their abilities to participate.

As indicated by the Gelmon study, our partnership was an organic, living collective. Distinctively, our mission—to foster a community-centric, multicultural teacher education—demanded attention to issues of race, culture, and power. Concern with difference and equality was woven into the fabric of our relationship. As examples, our partnership was a culturally and socially diverse coalition. Within the partnership, it was important to respect cultural diversity and to balance power. Further, the products of our partnership, from service-learning tasks to their evaluation, were a living testament to principles of multicultural education.

Service learning usually is located in communities of color or in economic distress. Teacher educators and service learners, in contrast, are privileged by employment and attendance at colleges and universities. Answers to "Where's the community in service-learning research?" need to attend explicitly to differences in power among these groups, to coalition across race, social class, and privilege, and to the concerns raised by such alliance.

THE SPIRIT OF SHARED CONTROL

Most literature emphasizes impacts of service learning upon service learners. The views shared here suggest that community service learning motivated, engaged, and gratified community leaders and tapped into resources of local community associations. This partnership represents an incomparable moment in time. Yet, the principles of genuine partnership—reciprocity, mutuality, and empowerment—remain and bear repetition. These notions need further study among other partnerships shaped by cultural diversity and attentive to issues of equality and equity.

The integration of community-based service learning and multi-cultural education is a novel discourse (O'Grady, 2000). The perceptions of this partnership enrich this discussion. The tone of partners' remarks is telling. There is a sense of fruitfulness that something significant happens that will positively influence the education of culturally diverse or low-income youth. This partnership is not the be-all and end-all of multicultural coalitions. Probably, aspects of inclusion or collaboration were overlooked. But, it submits an idea—shared control—that can invest and empower all parties.

Shared control is a spirit of commitment to collective endeavor. It is a faith in the value of diverse perspectives. It is a recognition of the strength of a pluralistic, university-community teaching coalition. This spirit emerged from and through a process of pedagogical decisions and applications, such as the construction and utilization of the task-based contract. In the next chapter, the ways in which shared control was exercised or practiced are explained and considered.

CHAPTER 6

The Exercise of Shared Control

What impressed me was the fact that perfect strangers came together and created a dialogue and learning project that best suited the academic needs of the students, without dissimulation or reservation. This is something you don't find everyday. On a daily basis, people exhibit prejudices based on fear. In our project, fear has been jailed. Love has risen to the surface. (W.M., research forum, 12/10/99)

During the fall of 1999, the director of the campus Office of Community Partnerships in Service Learning often sat in on class sessions and community meetings. On several occasions, I heard her describe the current service-learning project as a "good model" that deserved replication. I cringed whenever I heard this expression. To me, shared control for multicultural service learning is not a depersonalized, preset model, but rather a carefully nurtured nexus of relationships. It is *working with* representatives from culturally diverse and low-income communities as coeducators for future teachers—in all that this conviction implies. It is listening to alternative voices outside the usual confines of teacher education. It is commitment to joint development of the service-learning effort. It is distributed responsibility for oversight and evaluation of prospective teachers' work. It is dynamic, serendipitous, and interpersonal. In this chapter, one occasion to work with community partners is described: our move from "perfect strangers to educational partners" is recalled, our construction of a service-learning project is outlined, and our exercise of shared control is detailed.

FROM PERFECT STRANGERS
TO EDUCATIONAL PARTNERS

We were not really perfect strangers, we were more like limited associates. As described in Chapter 4, except for a presemester planning session, a class orientation event, and a debriefing luncheon, the parties to service learning did not commune regularly with one another. Instead of a communicative network, there was a two-way flow of information; directors of organizations and I talked about concerns with one another. Shared control demanded a decentered approach of multidirectional give-and-take. It called for more input from and interchange among previously quiet and distanced associates.

I wanted to ask more from my associates, but I hesitated to solicit more of their time, especially free of charge. I obtained a small research grant, just enough to provide stipends to offset my associates' time for extended summer meetings. Most community representatives donated the stipends to their organizations, but the monies demonstrated my respect for their expertise. During our summer mornings together, we renewed our acquaintance, clarified our aims and needs, and tested the waters of new ideas. My previously silent associates became close partners, and the notion of shared control took on a life of its own. Some simple questions guide this consideration of the exercise of shared control: What made it work? What kept it going?

SNAPSHOTS OF SHARED CONTROL

The exercise of shared control proceeded through two forms: dialogue and pedagogy. The partners deliberated and planned, then implemented and evaluated the service-learning exercise. Reams of data were collected about both forms, and I culled from them. I concentrated on illustrative moments that exemplified the quintessence of shared control. Summer meetings, as the initiation of dialogue and the construction of common cause, are detailed. Four teaching strategies, central to multicultural service learning, are delineated: (1) the task-based contract, an agreement between preservice teachers and community partners to complete five required activities for service learning; (2) reflective essays, three sets of writings by preservice teachers in response to guiding questions, with feedback from community partners and me; 3) reflective discussions, three class sessions devoted to reflection upon service-learning experiences, lead by community partners; and 4) mini-inquiries, limited field studies of questions which arose during service learning.

First, three summer meetings are described. Their agendas are recalled, and decisions made by the community partners are highlighted. Second, each of the four teaching strategies are presented. An authentic example demonstrates the strategy in action. Analysis of the specific example and general strategy follows. I selected exemplary moments through connoisseurship (Eisner, 1985), informed critique born of long-term association with the service-learning project. The intent is to provide snapshots that glimpse the exercise of shared control.

Construction of Common Cause

> Collaboration sounds like a good idea, but in this project we're really trying it. It really makes a community among all of us" (G.P., research forum, 9/8/99).

What was the genesis of shared control? The summer sessions were a key initiation to the attitude and aim of the project. The partnership group met for a morning in June, July, and August. Several community center directors were busy with summer youth camps, and their attendance was erratic. We kept in touch by sending them follow-up letters and packets of meeting materials. The meetings are described in some detail to get a feel for the construction of common cause.

Aims for the first meeting were to consider meanings of shared control and to suggest service-learning tasks responsive to community associations and beneficial for multicultural education. First, definitions of service learning were discussed. The partners agreed that an approach that balanced attention to both service and learning was germane to the project (Sigmon, 1994). Then, I proposed goals for multicultural service learning, such as develop positive, cross-cultural contacts, recognize children as cultural beings with various frames of reference, and acknowledge children's learning outside school. I sketched what an approach that was equally weighted between service and learning might look like: preservice teachers assisting organizations with temporary, programmatic needs, and community organizations aiding future teachers in learning about youth, families, and local concerns. The partners then brainstormed activities that balanced service and learning and made sense for their particular organizations. The group decided to collaborate on three undertakings: to designate a set of service-learning tasks, to construct a contractual agreement for service learning, and to develop evaluative criteria for service-learning efforts.

Prior to the second meeting, I prepared a sample, task-based contract, as a starting point for our discussions. The sample included a letterhead that introduced us, for the first time, as Community Partners. This identification silently validated shared leadership. I also drafted a service-learning syllabus and timeline, and I made copies of a mini-inquiry project, previously used as a capstone for service learning.

The majority of the morning was spent mulling over the task-based contract. The partners added specificity to the utilization of field hours:

5 of 20 hours were designated for observation, 15 of 20 were allotted to task completion. Community partners suggested options, workable for their sites, within general categories of tasks. For example, in order to learn about family values and concerns, preservice teachers could assist as a home-based tutor or observe a home visit. As part of the service-learning syllabus, the group developed a five-question framework for reflective essays. In a spirit of wholehearted commitment, partners volunteered to give feedback on three sets of essays written by service learners assigned to their organizations. The group endorsed the mini-inquiry as a final project, and association directors agreed to guide the inquiry, particularly to arrange for in-group (local) interviews.

For the third meeting, I brought copies of an introductory letter for the project, updated drafts of service-learning and multicultural education course syllabi, and university evaluation forms for service-learning courses. The itinerary was hefty. We added more information about community organizations to the introductory letter. We reviewed the syllabi and determined procedures and time frames for service-learning activities. We considered community participation in reflective class sessions and decided to rotate leadership, with at least two partners in charge of each session. At my urging, the group entertained the notion of reflection upon and writing about our venture (the research forums and coauthorship of Chapter 5 sprang from this dialogue). As a final item, we planned an orientation for service learning, to be held during a meeting of the multicultural education class.

The orientation took place in early September (see Figure 6.1). A sense of expectation rippled through the university classroom. All of the community partners were in attendance. Preservice teachers were anxious to meet their local community instructors for the first time. I introduced the partners as coteachers or community instructors. I talked a bit about our good fortune to work with cultural brokers to a local neighborhood and to a culturally diverse population. Each partner outlined his or her hopes and plans for service learning. I then provided an overview of the project, retracing in brief the partner's discussions and decisions during the summer. A balanced approach to service and learning was described, multicultural service learning was defined, and potential field tasks were suggested. Afterward, partners met with their site-based teams and oriented them to customs and codes of conduct for their organizations. The orientation packed a punch: it introduced the format for multicultural service learning, showcased community instructors, set parameters for on-site behavior, and emphasized local endorsement of the project.

The summer and orientation meetings constituted common cause and fostered communal identification. Previously, I did not work with com-

FIGURE 6.1: Orientation to Community Service Learning

Community partners
- Lynne Boyle-Baise, Multicultural Teacher Education
- William McCoy, Anointed Harvest Fellowship Church
- Joni Clark and Gwen Paulk, Bethel AME Church
- Bart Epler, Boys and Girls Club
- Chris Truelock, Banneker Westside Community Center
- Nancy Slough, Head Start

Reasons for community-based service learning as part of multicultural education
- Teachers and students are cultural beings; cultural differences can be source of misunderstandings.
- Academic learning is based on prior learning, much of which occurs outside school.
- Community learning can provide opportunities for cross-cultural interaction.
- Service learning provides reasons for being in community; it encourages reflection on experience.

Types of Service Learning (based on Sigmon, 1994)	
service LEARNING	learning goals primary, service outcomes secondary
SERVICE learning	service outcomes primary, learning goals secondary
service learning	service and learning goals completely separate
SERVICE LEARNING	service and learning goals of equal weight, each enhance the other–for all participants

How can we structure service and learning in ways that
- respond to real needs of community organization,
- build trust and respect for others,
- gain understanding of the lives (attitudes, values, routines, concerns) of children and families, and
- introduce the issues and concerns of the local community?

Service
- Assist in organization and implementation of a special project or event
- Assist in ongoing programs; tutor, teacher's aide, playground assistant

Learning
- Tutor an individual: visit his or her family, find out about learning preferences and needs
- Attend parent or board meetings: participate as secretary or some support role

Our plans
- Task-based contract
- Reflective essays
- Reflective class sessions

Meetings with community instructors

munity liaisons as a group to explore assumptions, concur on definitions, or shape the character of multicultural service learning. The clarification process created a basis for mutual understanding and collective effort. The notion of partnership moved from an abstraction to a reality. Through conversation, suggestion, and debate the outline of a community-based educational endeavor formed within a pluralistic group.

Teaching Tools

> To have more hands on with the contracts, our meetings, seeing what everybody thinks, brainstorming together. That's positive. (B.E., research forum, 9/8/99)

Task-Based Contract. The contract established a compact between the preservice teacher and the community instructor (see Figure 6.2). Prospective teachers promised to complete five major tasks for service learning, and community instructors agreed, in return, to supervise and assist them. Preservice teachers completed three of the four following tasks: assist as a tutor, mentor, or teacher's aide; attend a parent or board meeting; participate in a special site event; and interact with one family in depth. They also conducted a limited field study and reflected upon their learning via three reflective essays. The contract was deemed a blueprint or guide by community partners (see Chapter 5). It set parameters, but allowed for variation within task categories. It held both parties, community instructors and preservice teachers, accountable to prespecified, clear, consistent expectations.

The task-based contract probably operated most meaningfully when I was not there to see it. Preservice teachers referred to it frequently in the field. The contract served as a handy pocket map, which clearly outlined the dimensions of multicultural service learning. At midterm, the partners met to assess the project. A major discussion item was completion of the task-based contract. Several partners were startled to find the semester half gone and many tasks undone. Others felt right on target. Regardless, the group concluded that the tasks and timetable were feasible. Partners described their accomplishment of several tasks, for instance, preservice teachers had chaperoned youth on a field trip, accompanied teachers on home visits, or participated in a Family Skate Night. No major modifications were proposed for the contract—it stood as is.

Although common in structure, completed contracts reveal a range of actual service-learning activities. For example, for the task category "assistance as a tutor or mentor," preservice teachers taught Sunday School, instituted a tutoring program, implemented a reading incentive program,

FIGURE 6.2: Task-Based Contract

Community partners
- Lynne Boyle-Baise, Multicultural Teacher Education
- William McCoy, Anointed Harvest Fellowship Church
- Joni Clark and Gwen Paulk, Bethel AME Church
- Bart Epler, Boys and Girls Club
- Chris Truelock, Banneker Westside Community Center
- Nancy Slough, Head Start

One credit is earned for the completion of the following:
- Observe and participate for 20 hours at a community site
  (15 of 20 hours should be used to complete the task-based contract)
- Complete task-based contract: *complete 3 of first 4 tasks*
- Conduct a mini-inquiry into a question relevant to your site
- Write three essays in which you reflect upon your activities
- Participate in reflective class sessions.

Service-Learning Tasks				
General task	Specific description	Time in/out	Date completed	Signature of supervisor
Assist as tutor, mentor, or teacher's aide				
Attend a parent or board meeting				
Attend a special site event or field trip				
Interact with one family in depth (tutor, shadow, or home visit)				
Complete a mini-inquiry project				
Write three reflective essays				

I agree to complete the tasks listed to earn one credit for service learning.

Name: _____ Date: _____

I agree to supervise this preservice teacher during the service-learning experience.

Name: _____ Date: _____

or organized a Hallelujah Party. Events that fostered close acquaintance with youth and families included: assistance with a "pumpkin pick," child care during a parent meeting, help with a fall carnival, and participation in an overnight "lock-in." The mini-inquiries, also called Why?-Studies, touched upon an assortment of family and community issues: Why does a church that is so culturally diverse work? Why are parents involved in Head Start? How does Boys and Girls Club impact the local community?

The task-based contract was central to shared control and fundamental to multicultural service learning. It set parameters that underscored aims for multicultural education. It allocated power for field-based teaching to community instructors. It increased community instructors' sense of responsibility for the day-to-day process of service learning. It pushed preservice teachers beyond tutoring roles to activities that afforded more complex understandings of community organizations and contexts. Moreover, during the completion of tasks, a wealth of teaching and learning opportunities arose. Discussion of the contract as a linear series of tasks belies the richness of these teachable moments. The following story glimpses the task-based contract at work and sketches an exchange between preservice teachers and their community instructor.

The Ladies Auxiliary for Boys and Girls Club organized a field trip to a pumpkin patch. Many brought their own children along to share the fun. When snack time came, some mothers directed their youngsters to a picnic table apart from club participants. Several put their children last in line, then explained, loud enough for all to hear, that club participants were poor, lacked sufficient food, and needed priority for snacks. Preservice teachers were upset. They felt club youth were ostracized and treated as charitable cases. Later, as part of another contract task, preservice teachers attended a board of directors meeting for the club. They were surprised to see (what they called) "suits" and "pearls," or white, middle-class professionals, in charge.

The site-based team brought their concerns to a reflective class session, attended by their community instructor. They wondered why parents of club participants and other adults from the neighborhood were not more involved in activities or in leadership. Their community instructor explained that the board and auxiliary members were comprised of people able to commit time to volunteer work. Often, parents were unable to leave their jobs in order to participate in club events. The class puzzled through several possibilities for greater inclusion of parents in the club. One suggestion was to reschedule events and meetings outside common work hours. Another was to invite parents to serve in leadership positions. Although seeds of systemic analysis of inequity lay in this example, the reflective exchange stopped short of this type of interrogation.

Reflective Essays. Preservice teachers wrote three essays in which they reflected upon their service-learning experiences. The directions for the essays were fairly simple. Preservice teachers were asked to write an essay that explored their learning. The following guiding questions were proposed:

- What events or ideas, if any, called forth an intellectual or emotional response?
- What, if anything, have I learned about funds of knowledge for teaching?
- Have my views, particularly about the labeling of others, changed in any way?
- Have my beliefs or views of myself changed in any way?
- What questions do I have for my community instructor?

As noted, partners agreed to read each set of essays and provide feedback. I viewed their readings as a wonderful opportunity for preservice teachers to experience other, diverse perspectives. For my partners, it also was an indicator of how preservice teachers viewed their service-learning experiences. As described in Chapter 5, in my partners' eyes the essays really "let us know where they are and what they learned" (W.M., research forum, 12/10/99). They served as a good evaluation of service learners' thinking and presented opportunities for guidance. Feedback from the partners was rich and varied, some wrote lengthy letters or painstaking memos, others commented briefly in margins and at the end of essays. Partners provided a multicultural education as they questioned bias, presumption, or cultural misinformation.

I provided feedback on reflective essays as well. Preservice teachers were afforded two lenses to inform their thinking. Additionally, they witnessed another community link, between their professor and their community instructors. We built community through our service as coteachers, amply illustrated through joint review of reflective essays.

Feedback from one partner, an education director for a predominately black church, to a white preservice teacher under her tutelage is illustrative. Over the three required reflective essays, the community instructor guides the preservice teacher through a process of waking up.

Essay #1. In the first essay, the instructor disrupts stereotypes, challenges assumptions, and compliments the preservice teacher on her forthright approach to learning. Through her feedback, the community instructor helps to dispute deficit views held by the preservice teacher.

The preservice teacher wrote: "I used to think Blacks were Baptist and they were always in church all day long" (J.C., 9/24/99). The community instructor noted in the margin: "Hopefully, this experience is helping you break down this stereotype" (G.P., 9/29/99). The preservice teacher wrote: "black people think it is important for children to be part of the church as they grow, seeing the spirit and responsibilities of the people of God." The instructor noted in the margin: "Don't whites?" At the essay's end, the instructor remarked: "I noticed that many of your comments lump all African Americans into one common group. As there is diversity in white culture, the same holds true for African Americans." The instructor encouraged the preservice teacher to "avoid assumptions." She then congratulated the preservice teacher on her frankness and suggested that she could learn a lot at the church.

Essay #2. In the second essay, the community instructor continues to prod the preservice teacher to grapple with stereotypes. The instructor helps the preservice teacher make connections between her momentary feeling of invisibility and the disregard often experienced by African Americans. (Recall that making connections was one developmental category of the Boyle-Baise/Sleeter conceptual framework, outlined in Chapter 3.) The instructor then suggests avenues for further learning—readings and cross-cultural interactions. Her suggestions nudge the preservice teacher from deficit to affirmative, social-change-oriented views.

The preservice teacher wrote: "I am experiencing the black people's culture, which in some ways is similar to mine, but with differences that can only be observed when spending time with them" (J.C., 10/15/99). The instructor noted: "Using the word 'the' gives me the feeling that you view black people as objects instead of people who are of a different race and culture than you. Just say black people" (G.P., 10/20/99). The preservice teacher wrote: "Just because I was the only white person there did not mean I should feel bad. I did notice that many people look at black people only and tend to look past me." The instructor responded: "Ralph Ellison writes about this in his book *The Invisible Man*. This happens to blacks by whites quite often." At the essay's end, the instructor remarked: "I can see that through this experience you are 'waking up.' I believe it is affecting everything you know and value. You are receiving a lot of truths." The instructor recommended reading Ellison's book and interacting with African American university students outside the church setting.

Essay #3. In the third essay, the preservice teacher dares to confront her own racism. She also recognizes and probes her ethnic identity. The instructor retains her direct, frank, helpful stance. She continues to augment the multicultural education this preservice teacher receives. Moreover, a level of trust is evident. A cross-cultural relationship has been developed that demonstrates community-building as a direct, person-to-person link. The community instructor offers friendship and mentorship, beyond the limits of multicultural service learning.

The preservice teacher wrote: "It's not that I was racist before, but those notions influenced my thoughts as I grew up. Things stayed in my mind because nobody challenged them, or maybe because I did not make the effort to change them" (J.C., 11/5/99). The community instructor noted in the margin: "You probably had unintentional racist notions before this experience. You are now learning about self and others" (G.P, 11/10/99). The preservice teacher wrote: "Being white is an ethnicity too; if we forget who we are, it can be hard to mix with others. It is important to be confident in one's own culture before learning a new one." The instructor responded: "Black people have believed this for years, but whites have a hard time understanding this!" At essay's end, the instructor added: "The project is about over, but our friendship doesn't have to be. Keep learning, stay open-minded to new experiences and cultures. You'll do fine."

Reflective Class Sessions. Three 2-hour class sessions were reserved for reflection. In order to share control, at least two community partners served as coteachers and led reflective discussions. At these moments, community interests entered most vibrantly into the classroom. A multicultural education was invigorated through a touchstone with real community life. During reflective sessions, authentic incidents spawned discussions of culture, equality, and equity. These discussions offered occasions for praxis, the linkage of cultural realizations to future teaching practice. Reflective sessions were a fundamental aspect of teacher preparation for change making in schools. In the following two snapshots, real events spur preservice teachers to examine their assumptions and to consider the impact of community on children's lives.

Reflective Class Discussion #1. Community Teachers: Bart Epler, Boys and Girls Club; Reverend Joni Clark, Bethel African Methodist Episcopal (AME) Church.

In this first snapshot, deficit views of parental care are challenged. What it means to know the whereabouts of one's children after school is reconsidered. A community instructor volunteers an insider's view of safety in this low-income neighborhood, and she is supported by a preservice teacher who lives there. Preservice teachers are encouraged to rethink their assumptions about after-school care and about being at home in this neighborhood.

Preservice Teacher 1: The community center is so unstructured.
    Sometimes only a few kids are there. I guess these parents are

working so much, they don't keep tabs on where their kids are.

Bart: They are neighborhood kids. They are within walking distance. At Boys and Girls Club, we do transportation. We bring kids to us. It is still nice out. When it gets cold, more kids will come.

Lynne: Reverend Clark, you live and work in that neighborhood. Can you help us understand how parents approach after-school care?

Reverend Clark: My daughter is 15. She gets out of school at 2:30 p.m. I know that between 2:30 and 3:00 she should be at home or somewhere in the neighborhood. I don't know where she is at the exact minute. The community is so small, someone knows where they are. The kids may not be at the center, it may not seem structured. The fact that they have that place, they can check in, is a wonderful thing. Sometime during the week, they will check in, if only out of curiosity. Kids know if the need arises they can go to the center. Kids do other after-school activities too. You have to know your community before you can say why kids aren't there.

Lynne: Many people think the neighborhood is not safe. Yet, Reverend Clark finds it a place where people know each other's children and feel safe when their children are there.

Preservice Teacher 2: I live in that neighborhood. A week ago a little girl was crying on the corner late at night because her mom was not home. My roommate and I went to help her. About four other neighbors came out and helped her find her mom. The neighbors got the situation under control.

Reflective Class Discussion #2. Community Teachers: Gwen Paulk, Bethel AME Church; Chris Truelock, Banneker Westside Community Center.

In this second snapshot, a neighborhood issue with cultural, social, and historic overtones is explored. Community instructors share their consternation over the issue. Preservice teachers are alerted to the presence of big-city problems in small towns and to the importance of knowing about the local concerns of neighborhoods in which they will work.

Lynne: Preservice Teacher 1 said she did not think small towns had racial problems or gang issues, yet she found out there was an issue with "the wall." Now she wonders if small towns have these concerns too. What is the problem with the wall and how does it inform you as future teachers?

Chris: Gwen is on our advisory board. We have struggled with this. A brief history of the wall is this: there is a limestone wall that surrounds the center. It was built by the WPA in 1936. As years have gone by, generations have hung out on that wall. If we take it away, it takes something of the neighborhood away. But now we have run into big-city issues. We have gang-bangers [gang members] hanging out on the wall. People are being harassed, there is a lot of smoking, some vandalism. There is some drug dealing too. It has come to the point where we need to make a stand. We don't want to kick the kids off the wall. We don't want to see them leave and just go elsewhere.

Preservice Teacher 2: Are kids hanging out on the wall instead of coming into the center?

Chris: I think they should be inside, working on their character, their homework, and becoming a better person. If they want to smoke, swear, or cut up, which we don't allow in the center, then they do it on that wall. The reason it has come to a head is that they are influencing our younger kids. That is just not going to happen.

Gwen: At the same time, we have to be sensitive to the culture of the wall, to the parents and grandparents who hung out at that wall. They feel very strongly about the significance of the wall for that neighborhood. Some people believe that at least if these children are on the wall, they are in the neighborhood where someone can keep an eye on them. But the eyes are not being kept on them because problematic things are going on.

Lynne: How can teachers learn about things like the wall in their school neighborhoods?

Preservice Teacher 2: We could get involved in an advisory board for a community center.

Preservice Teacher 3: Could the center hold a forum, like a town meeting, and let people know what's up? Then teachers could attend.

Gwen: The public is invited to board meetings. For lack of time or interest we haven't had any visitors.

Chris: We have a fairly good relationship established with certain teachers and the principal at the neighborhood school. There are phone calls constantly going back and forth. . . . The question you need to ask is how committed are you going to be to these kids' lives? There is no reason why you can't find out what goes on in their lives after school or call parents every night.

As these excerpts show, reflection was key to quality multicultural service learning. Two fundamental aspects of multicultural service learning, building community and questioning inequality, are demonstrated in these excerpts. Deficit views of low-income neighborhoods are challenged, and instead, local concerns are considered from insiders' perspectives. Preservice teachers are encouraged to inform their teaching through community connections, and the neighborhood center is identified as a community asset. Preservice teachers are not allowed to denigrate parents or find low-income locales inherently unsafe. Instead, these bases for lowered expectations, a form of educational inequality, are questioned.

Reflective discussions varied in their moments of intensity for multicultural service learning. I invited community partners-instructors to pose discussion questions. Some partners raised more provocative issues than others. Commonly, they asked, How is service learning going so far? This query brought forth compliments and complaints. Questions that prompted dialogue about culture and power included: What were your expectations going into service learning? Did your expectations differ from reality? What are the needs and values of the families at your organization? How does your organization serve as a teaching resource?

The partners' questions usually got to the heart of concerns for multicultural education. My role was one of secondary leadership. I attempted to probe field incidents for concerns with equality and equity. Commonly, interactions were less critical of systemic ills than I had hoped. Yet, community building, in communitarian and social change senses were demonstrated. Shared control was played out as collective leadership for reflective discussions. The capacities of community people and assets of communities were accentuated. Further, culture and race were primary foci of reflections, not side issues. I could and should have built upon reflective discussions with subsequent attention to systemic inequality.

Mini-Inquiry Projects. The mini-inquiry project was also called a Why?-study. It was an opportunity for preservice teachers to investigate a question of why, what, or how that arose during multicultural service learning, in relation to concepts studied in the multicultural education class. Ideally, the question represented a bonafide puzzlement prompted by sustained time in a local milieu. The study went beyond traditional library research to focus on information-gathering techniques: interviews, observations, and document collection. Field-based study was undertaken with two ends in mind: to prod preservice teachers to seek and listen to local, insider (in-group) perspectives; and to practice a viable form of inquiry for learning about their future students. (An in-group informant is a member of a group under study.) For the assignment sheet for the mini-inquiry see Figure 6.3.

FIGURE 6.3: Mini-Inquiry Project

The purpose of this project is to investigate a question that emerges from your community service-learning experience. The research must include in-group (relevant to the question asked) perspectives and library research. It should be done with a partner(s) from your service-learning site. It can be completed as a videotape or a paper. Plan to present your research on [date]. Develop a summary sheet about your project to share with the class.

Each project should include the following:

1. *Introduction:* what your question is, what the inquiry is going to cover

2. *Research:* what you found out about your question, what you learned from in-group interviews, collection of on-site documents, and library research

3. *Analysis:* links between your findings and concepts learned in the multicultural education class

4. *Conclusions:* what you learned that relates to your future teaching, what you learned about doing inquiry related to teaching

5. *Additional questions:* what questions remain, what you would like to learn more about

6. *References:* list references (people, documents, books, and so on) for your investigation

The following criteria are suggested for evaluation of the project:

1. *Scholarly knowledge base of inquiry:* Are in-group sources used? Does library research support your inquiry?

2. *Multicultural perspectives:* Are multiple points of view included?

3. *Level of analysis:* Do you clearly and fully consider your findings in light of what we learned in the multicultural education class?

4. *Completeness of conclusions:* Do you thoughtfully consider what your findings mean for your teaching and for the completion of research related to your teaching?

The mini-inquiry was initiated through a proposal process, much like more advanced field research. The proposal format was brief, but afforded an opportunity for community instructors and me to discuss intended projects with service-learning teams. I pushed teams to clarify and narrow their questions or to link them more closely with concepts considered in the multicultural education course. Preservice teachers commonly studied ways in which community associations served as local assets. This thrust was supported, and sometimes suggested, by community instructors. As part of the proposal process, partners aided in the recruitment of adult, in-group, interview respondents. For example, in order to assist preservice teachers in their investigation of parent involvement in Head Start, the community instructor introduced them to parents willing to take part in an interview. Usually, community partners also served as key informants. As a demonstration of shared control, the community instructor and I signed the proposal form, indicating approval for the study. For the proposal form, see Figure 6.4.

A videotaped or traditional paper version of the inquiry was acceptable. Four of five service-learning teams chose the video option. The fifth group developed a simple survey to gather information from parents (the in-group for their question), then completed a traditional paper. Several teams supplemented video presentations with short reports of their library research. All of the groups turned in documents collected from their sites as part of their data.

The mini-inquiry of the team located at Boys and Girls Club clearly was outstanding. It was not their approach to field study that was especially distinctive. Their research proposal, like most, was sketchy, but useable. Their focus was interesting, but not critical. It was the verve with which they confronted and completed the inquiry that stood apart. Their research question was, How does the Boys and Girls Club impact the local community? The following snapshot offers a glimpse of the inquiry process at its moment of conclusion.

Imagine a videotaped presentation of research. The camera zooms in on two anchorwomen for a television newscast. The set depicts an urban, high-rise landscape, with Channel E300 (the multicultural education course number) boldly emblazoned across the top. In the background, a narrator's voice introduces viewers to "your favorite show about cultural diversity." One of the anchors explains: "We will be reporting live from various places that have a positive effect on our community. Today, we are on-site at Boys and Girls Club." A second anchor exhibits a pamphlet about the club, reads its mission statement, and delineates its various activities. Then the view changes to a live, on-the-scene report.

FIGURE 6.4: Proposal Form

Mini-Inquiry Project

Partners: _____

1. What is your proposed area of inquiry? What is your main question?

2. Who is your in-group for your question? Who do you plan to interview?

3. What interview questions do you plan to ask?
   (Limit 2–3 questions, 15-minute interviews)

4. What library research will help you answer your question?
   (Specify books, videos, and so on)

5. How will you organize the work of your project?
   (Who will do what, when?)

6. What questions do you have about your research project?

7. What help, if any, do you need to get started?

Signature of Community Instructor: _____

Signature of University Instructor: _____

A field reporter interviews the core services director. He asks the director to describe her job, to consider the club's influence on the community, and to indicate ways in which the club promotes diversity. The core services director then leads the reporter on an annotated tour of club facilities. Subsequent scenes shift back and forth from the anchors to the scene as the program director (also the community partner-instructor) and the individual services director (social worker) are interviewed according to the same format, and snippets of youth participation in the club are shown. The anchors invite the audience to utilize or assist the club, provide contact information to do so, and sign off. As a supplement to their video presentation, the team refers their classmates to the annual report for the Boys and Girls Club. They catalog ways in which the club invests in local youth, and they accent the provision of "positive developmental, educational, and recreational programs for girls and boys."

After the research presentation, I questioned the team about what they learned, particularly about their emphasis on the need for positive after-school youth programs. I wondered how their findings might impact their future teaching. Each member proposed heightened teacher concern with students' lives after school. This remark is illustrative:

> The individual services director told us that trouble hours for kids are between 3 and 6. You never think about that. As a teacher you think your job is done at 3:00, but you still need to worry about your students. It is important for teachers to tell parents about Boys and Girls Club as a safe, low-cost, after-school program. And, talk to the club to see how teachers can work with it. (A.M., 12/8/99)

The team's community instructor then shared his views. He echoed the need for positive after-school youth options and for teachers to become engaged in local programs: "With youth, you have to have positive involvement. . . . We don't have enough teachers come over. As a teacher, try to collaborate with the youth organizations. The Boys and Girls Club needs to collaborate more with teachers too" (B.E., 12/8/99).

The primary purpose of the mini-inquiry was to investigate questions related to the service-learning experience. This aim was met, yet inquiries tended to skirt root causes for social problems. Instead, the mini-inquiries tended to describe, then applaud, intervention programs. For example, programs at the Boys and Girls Club were praised as beneficial for potentially troubled youth. Preservice teachers did not probe the kind of programs deemed positive, the form of trouble expected, or the relation of problems to larger issues of racism or poverty. This shortcoming does not, necessarily, suggest a flaw in the mini-inquiry project. It indicates that preservice teachers needed more understanding and practice of social or institutional critique. Service learning can, however, pose barriers to systemic critique. If community associations emphasize programmatic resolutions to racism or poverty, then preservice teachers likely will find meliorative approaches entirely appropriate.

Another aim of the mini-inquiry was to teach prospective teachers to conduct field research as a tool for learning about students, families, and communities. This objective largely was met. Preservice teachers practiced ethnographic investigation, complete with in-group interviews, participant observations, and collection of documents (e.g., organizational pamphlets). Study of secondhand library resources supplemented field research. As part of their conclusions, teams considered the impact of what they learned upon their future teaching. Inquiry was approached as a basis for decision making in the classroom. Thus, field-based study was practiced as a tool for change making in schools.

Getting through the process of a field study was daunting. I wonder if the ends justified the means. Preservice teachers practiced quite a few research techniques, but their topics of study were fairly bland. Sometimes less is more. A less broad form of field study, say a case study of a youngster's life after school, might have practiced inquiry and focused more intimately on one's future students, their families, and communities.

THE EXERCISE OF SHARED CONTROL

Responsibility for the program does not fall on anyone's part. It is dispersed between us, even grading. We can make changes. It all helps the program. (W.M., research forum, 9/8/99)

Shared control: What makes it work, what keeps it going? In order to puzzle through these questions, I crawl inside this instance of shared control and search for its scaffolding. I deconstruct it, if you will. I locate shared control at the intersection of communitarian and social change endeavors. For multicultural service learning, both the construction of conjoint efforts and their embodiment as affirmative regard for diversity and pluralism are needed. I find four interrelated, undergirding dimensions at this intersection: the development of common purpose, the cultivation of a free interplay of ideas, the unfolding of true dialogue, and the enactment of passions of pluralism. These impulses, arguably, made shared control work and kept it going.

Common Purpose

I referred to John Dewey's democratic ideal in Chapter 2. Ideally, democracy is perceived as more than a distanced government; rather it is a form of associated living. Citizens can work together to improve their lives. They can deliberate about public affairs, open to hearing other's views and to reconsidering their own. Based on thoughtful give-and-take, citizens can construct mutual interests and purposes. A sense of community is cultivated through conjoint endeavor. What undergirds the development of a collective sense of purpose? Dewey (1916/1966) proposes the following two criteria for the democratic ideal:

> Now in any social group whatever, even in a gang of thieves, we find some interest held in common, and we find a certain amount of interaction and cooperative intercourse with other groups. From these two traits, we derive our standard. How numerous and varied are the interests which are consciously shared? How full and free is the interplay with other forms of association? (p. 83)

This group of university and community people held interests in common, enriched by varied personal views. The partnership group jointly envisioned more equal, excellent, and equitable education for all children, particularly for youth from ethnic minority or low-income groups, historically ill-served by public schools. Our partnership offered an opportunity for community input into the preparation of teachers who would serve children like the community's own. Although we coalesced around this aim, our different perspectives broadened and deepened it. For example, for the pastor of the AME church, the service-learning project offered occasions for youth to interact with future teachers, outside school, on equal footing. For the parent coordinator at Head Start, the project afforded a glimpse of social work in support of children from low-income homes. Our views reflected our lived experiences as educators, parents, organization directors, or ministers, as members of ethnic majority or minority groups, and as insiders or outsiders to the locus for service learning.

This group of university and community people also interacted across associations. Previously, the several partnership organizations were loosely connected; there was little interplay among them. For example, the parent coordinator at Head Start noted that before this project she did not know what went on at other social agencies, but now she personally knew directors of several community service organizations. At this juncture, we met together around the same table with time for dialogue and deliberation. The structure we proposed benefited from interplay across organizational groups. For example, we realized that the task-based contract needed to flex to encompass aims and activities of different associations. Also, the entire group of preservice teachers were exposed to multiple stances of various community partners through their joint participation in reflective class discussions.

Through the process of interchange, partners learned from one another. We gained knowledge of goals, concerns, and achievements of various community organizations. We shared concerns and swapped ideas. For example, at our midterm meeting, we discussed our progress with the task-based contract. The program director at the Boys and Girls Club described his interpretation of one task, the in-depth interaction with youth and family. He insisted that members of his service-learning team ride the club bus, at least once, as it picked up youth from school. Preservice teachers sat and talked casually with children; particularly they asked about children's school day. The education director for the AME church wondered how this idea might translate to her setting. She decided to invite parents to be shadowed for a typical day; preservice teachers could converse casually with them and their children as they went about routines. Basically, we formed a network of organizational involvement in service learning. Our complex partnership afforded an amplified approach to service learning.

Free Interplay of Ideas

Dewey (1916/1966) speaks to the power of ideas, potentially developed within culturally diverse coalitions. He proposes that a "free play back and forth" (p. 84) of ideas can mitigate one-sidedness and stimulate diverse perspectives. According to Dewey, an extension in the number of individuals who participate in an interest, and the proliferation and consideration of views thereof, can break down "barriers of class, race, and national territory" (p. 87).

This partnership was not large in number, comprised of seven individuals, but it was notably diverse. Five members were parents, three with children in local schools; three members were African American, four were European American, four were women, three were men; four members lived in or attended church in the local neighborhood; and two were long-time agency directors there. Only I, as a university teacher-educator, was a total outsider. This group offered potential for the proliferation of a diverse set of ideas. For example, as part of our feedback on reflective essays, community partners and I tackled issues of culture and race, but from different standpoints. I offered perceptions of a community outsider, a teacher from a majority ethnic group. Other partners provided views of community insiders, parents and leaders from majority and minority ethnic groups. Arguably, the endorsement of multiple perspectives mitigated one-sidedness.

This group aimed for partnership and operated on parity. Partnership meant full participation, shared commitments, and balanced obligations. As part of a multicultural education, the partnership also validated cultural and social diversity. Each partner took great pains to honor others' views and value others' expertise. For example, I recognized community partners as coteachers. In return, they appreciated my knowledge of multicultural education. Mutual respect and regard supported a "free back and forth of ideas." For example, I perceived grading as based on academic merit. Some of my partners centered evaluation around personal qualities like responsibility and dependability. Evaluation that focused on one without the other was lopsided. Our future practice benefits from this interchange of views. The impact of pluralism and parity on the exchange of ideas cannot be overstated. Our partnership embodied a coming together across barriers of race, social class, religion, profession, and institution.

True Dialogue

Lisa Delpit (1995) cautions that dialogue about education often is one-sided. The views of people of color are underrated or dismissed by white educators. She argues that ethnic minority groups are silenced by a "culture of power" (p. 24), or rules and codes of the dominant cultural group. She suggests that those in power, by virtue of their position and resources, frequently are least aware of or likely to disrupt their privilege. Delpit calls upon educators to initiate "true dialogue" by "seeking out those whose perspectives . . . differ most, by learning to give their words complete attention, by understanding one's own power . . . by being unafraid to raise questions about discrimination and voicelessness with people of color, and to . . . hear what they say" (p. 47).

Arguably, commitment to and practice of shared control unsettled the culture of power. I relinquished control for part of my multicultural education course, and my partners took it up. For example, community coteachers took charge of reflective class sessions. I played a supportive role, incorporating multicultural education concepts into discussions where appropriate. As another example, topics for mini-inquiries were shaped and approved by community partners, as well as by me. Collaboration has a nice, friendly feel to it, but in this case it exemplified a redistribution of power. What I want to call a nexus of relationships actually disrupted standard teacher education. I was not the sole arbiter of preservice teachers' educations, nor was the university classroom their primary source of information. The construction of these relationships acknowledges the worth of community-based learning and of community people as teacher educators.

For a long time, I tried to invite community input into service learning. Until I began to contemplate a task-based contract (an idea borrowed from my university's school of business), I lacked a method to disperse power, yet still guide experience. The task-based contract allocated a teaching space to the community, but provided a framework for it. In fussing with the contract, trying to get it right, true dialogue emerged. Topics of

discussion touched upon issues of power and privilege. As examples, partners proposed that tutoring requests be initiated by parents to accentuate
their involvement in learning, urged that a question about labeling be
included in the guide for reflective essays, and requested that preservice
teachers refrain from note taking during home visits to respect family privacy. Each party heard what the other wanted and needed. Discussions
of the contract also spawned a new type of cross-group dialogue, community feedback on reflective essays.

Educators have been deaf to community views for so long that there
is skepticism about our intent to listen. As part of the designation of partners as coteachers, I tried to ensure that each partner was treated as a teaching colleague. For example, communication was close and regular; mail-
ings, E-mails, and phone calls were routine. Little things made a symbolic
difference: Advance parking stickers eased university visits; on-site deliv-
ery of reflective essays assisted feedback; and thank-you notes acknowledged unpaid, silent contributions. These actions signaled serious intent
to foster true dialogue.

That it took several years for me to reach the point of true dialogue is
worth mention. There is a huge difference between participation as an
invited guest, however honored, and as a coteacher. This conclusion seems
simple, but it allows full-blown incursion into one's territory as university professor. One's turf can be quick to defend, difficult to share.

Passions of Pluralism

Maxine Greene (1993) describes community affirmation of cultural
diversity as "passions of pluralism" (p. 13). Greene envisions the creation
of authentic public space where diverse people come together, face-to-face,
to articulate multiple concerns and construct common purposes. She proposes that citizens willing to cross cultural and social boundaries to listen
and care can respond to their concerns in ways that respect pluralism and
build community.

Within these snapshots of multicultural service learning, a small, diverse
group of men and women are pictured at work. They sit around a table on
a summer morning and ponder suitable tasks for service learning. They write
forthright feedback to reflective essays and return them to the instructor in
time for class. They conduct reflective class sessions and honestly put forth
their values and perspectives. They monitor task-based contracts and ensure
preservice teachers have a range of cross-cultural experiences. They help
future teachers rethink what it means to serve the public within a culturally diverse society. They push prospective teachers to "extend the reference to 'us' as far as we can" (Rorty, cited in Greene, 1993, p. 18).

Was this collective effort to share control for multicultural service learning an example of passions for pluralism? The effort certainly broke through "persisting either/ors" (Greene, 1988, p. 8), at least momentarily, to reconfigure teacher education. In a university classroom, an assorted group of community partners reshaped multicultural education through the incorporation of their perspectives and expertise. In field settings, a task-based contract stood as a constitution of common concern. This endeavor to share control for multicultural service learning developed trusted and close working relationships among a culturally diverse group of imperfect strangers. It propelled strangers to cross usual boundaries of geography, culture, race, and institution to collaborate without dissimulation or reservation. It advanced a multicultural service-learning project that confirmed community, diversity, and equality. It seems to qualify. Perhaps it was a rare moment. As Reverend McCoy suggested, "this is something you don't find everyday."

COMMUNITY-BUILDING

The exercise of shared control is not a preconfigured or determinate model. It is a special nexus of personal and pedagogical relationships. It is *working with* representatives from culturally diverse and low-income communities as coeducators for future teachers. In operation, *working with* means acting as a community of teachers, based on parity, pledged to joint responsibility, and committed to cultural diversity and equality.

This example demonstrates a community-building orientation. Moreover, it suggests an intersection between communitarian and social change views (see Chapter 2 for full explanation of this paradigm). As a communitarian impulse, this partnership evidences mutual regard, deliberation, openness, tolerance, and empathy. The partners created something together that, in their minds, had integrity for multicultural teacher education. The process of construction generated a sense of connectedness, an esprit d'corps, among participants. As a motivation for social change, this partnership affirms cultural diversity, demonstrates pluralism, and attends to issues of equality and equity.

Arguably, the service-learning project constructed by the partnership still was not critical enough. Considerations of discrimination, racism, and other forms of inequality skimmed the surface. Underlying societal and institutional causes for racism or poverty were barely questioned. This pedagogy offers abundant potential to communicate with and learn from people different from oneself, to dash deficit views, and to recognize assets within low-income communities. It is very difficult, almost insensitive, to critique programs of the organizations with which one partners. Such critique might seem to denigrate worthy local initiatives. Further, it is disingenuous to fault programs as limited interventions when multicultural service learning is a similar limited intervention in teacher education.

This instance of shared control is not exemplary; instead, it is intended to be illustrative. Description and analysis of this exercise hopefully will serve as a springboard for further thought, research, and practice. Shared control signifies a promise of full partnership between university and community participants in multicultural service learning. Its fruition depends upon the construction of common cause, the free exchange of ideas, the development of true dialogue, and the pursuit of passions for pluralism. The partnership worked to the extent that communal affiliation was built, teamwork was cultivated, responsibilities were shared, and issues of cultural difference and power were addressed forthrightly.

In the next chapter, my journey comes full circle. I look back upon it and ponder lessons learned. I study multicultural service learning as it impacted preservice teachers and community partners. I consider building upon strengths and reducing weaknesses of the work presented here. Then I look forward and suggest methods to further investigate multicultural service learning.

Looking Back, A Year Later: Ryan's Reflections

As I reflect back a year later on my services at the Boys and Girls Club, I look at where I was before I attended, the times I was there, and now the time apart from the club. Since then, I have seen myself grow stronger as a multicultural person and facilitator to the community. Through my visitations to the club, I gained a positive attitude toward all children and the community they live in. I became an instrumental part of the welfare of the Bloomington community. I also learned the importance of a safe and positive atmosphere for children when not in school or at home. This community-based project has greatly enriched my life and attitude as a future professional educator.

When I first attended the Boys and Girls Club, I was a little apprehensive. I actually thought that these children were going to be like the teens in the movie *Dangerous Minds*. Growing up all my life in predominately white, middle-class neighborhoods, this was a common stereotype that I made. Although some of the children did experience traumatic situations in their homes and school, my experience was very good. The students taught me a lot. When I say that the students have taught me, I don't necessarily mean educationally, but more reality and life situations. They have taught me never to expect the ordinary.

As teachers, we encourage and practice lifelong learning. As an educator, I feel the best way to encourage this practice is to learn from our students and about our students. By interacting with students outside of a school environment, I learned more about children of the age I want to teach. I learned more by listening and observing these children than by reading about them in a book. From this experience I learned there are numerous outside stimuli that can affect a child, which in turn influences the educational process.

Before I took part in the service-learning project, I never really associated myself with the community and sheltered myself within the confines of the university. However, I now look for things to take part in that will diversify myself, not only as an educator, but as an individual as well. Through this community service learning, I learned the more diverse I am as a person, the more knowledge-able and understanding I will be as an educator. I am now more comfortable being around a more diverse group of children and, in fact, welcome it. This experience has helped assist me in prepa-ration for the future challenges that I will face as a multicultural educator. (Ryan Mikus, essay, 10/20/2000)

Chapter 7

Lessons Learned,
Learning Lessons

At the end of the multicultural education course described in Chapters 5 and 6, the Office of Community Partnerships in Service Learning (at my university) did an independent assessment of the service-learning aspect of the course. Responses overwhelmingly were positive: over 90 percent of the class strongly recommended the course based on its service-learning component. As part of the assessment, preservice teachers were invited to describe benefits of and barriers to service learning. A majority considered deeper ties to the community, increased understanding of its concerns, and heightened connections with families as significant benefits. A fair number also identified application of course concepts, self-transformation, expansion of worldviews, and experience with youth and families outside schools as major advantages. The barriers mentioned by more than one person included transportation, communication, unfriendly staff members, and behavior of children.

Furthermore, at semester's end, preservice teachers and I discussed ways to include their voices and views in future service-learning research. Excitement bubbled about the potential of a small volunteer self-study group that could chronicle its views during service learning. Some preservice teachers wanted to act immediately on this suggestion. They volunteered to write reflective essays for inclusion in this book. I accepted their proposal. Almost a year later, as I began writing, I reiterated my invitation to publish their essays. Several preservice teachers sent short E-mail notes remembering the class fondly. Ryan, however, leader of the potential writing group, made good his promise. He sent me the essay that precedes this chapter. I utilize his essay mostly because it is candid, considerate, and eloquent. Also, it illustrates a process of self-transformation and community connection experienced by many of Ryan's white classmates. Ryan is gregarious, humorous, and assured enough to embrace what he does not know. In his willingness to make his learning public, Ryan stands apart.

Ryan's reflections reverberate with some of my aims for multicultural service learning, but not with others. His story underscores the "lessons learned" that form this chapter. However, Ryan's recollections are only half of the story. Within this book, two foci are presented: multicultural service learning as perceived and enacted by preservice teachers, on the one hand, and by community partners, on the other. In this chapter, I review the lessons learned from both groups and suggest new directions. Additionally, I ponder ways to research the process of multicultural service learning and put forth new ideas.

LESSONS LEARNED: PRESERVICE TEACHERS

Ryan's reflection features several theoretical, conceptual, and pragmatic points discussed in the following sections. His personal biography influences his perceptions of service learning. He enters the experience with deficit views, springing from his Eurocentric, middle-class upbringing. Service learning augments Ryan's multicultural education in several ways. He shifts from a deficit to an affirmative posture toward culturally diverse or low-income youth and toward the communities from which they come. He benefits from an authentic context for learning about his future students, and through service learning, he learns to expect diversity and to acknowledge community influences on youth's lives. Ryan barely addresses systemic inequality; he mentions possible trauma in children's lives, but shifts quickly back to his own learning. Ryan perceives the advantage of service learning primarily in terms of becoming a better teacher, defined as greater comfort with diverse students. He is open to learning more about cultural diversity and intends to seek occasions to do so.

Theories

Three theories of how multicultural service learning works for preservice teachers were posed earlier: (1) Prior life experience with cultural diversity or poverty impacts one's perceptions of multicultural service learning; (2) preservice teachers hold paradigmatic (not progressive) views; and (3) multicultural service learning supports conceptual shifts that affirm multicultural education. All three positions were supported by data in Chapter 3.

Prior life experience with cultural diversity or poverty mattered. Preservice teachers with little direct experience of cultural diversity, racial discrimination, or economic adversity came to service learning with deficit views of people different from themselves. Preservice teachers of color from segregated backgrounds held deficit views as well. Preservice teachers tended to shift toward more affirmative perspectives, but in different ways.

Most white preservice teachers perceived youth as "all alike," a stance of
equal regard which obscured real differences in life conditions. Many prospective teachers of color "made connections" between previous and current examples of denigration or bias, a stance which deepened their commitment to equality through education.

Preservice teachers tended to come to service learning with paradigmatic views, a set of beliefs and attitudes which undergirded their actions.
Most white preservice teachers shifted from a charitable, deficit orientation to liberal views, as defined by the civic education paradigm. They
intended to help all children have equal opportunities to learn. Most preservice teachers of color remained within a community-building/social
change paradigm, but deepened their understandings of it. They confronted
racial bias related to their segregated backgrounds, gained comfort in
mixed-race situations, and pondered meanings of equality in integrated
settings (see details of paradigms in Chapter 2).

A continuum of growth, as a signification of individual learning and
change (i.e., learners move from a personal link with someone in need to
a grasp of social problems, to a concern for societal justice), does not capture the multiple ways in which life conditions, social problems, and social justice are viewed. For example, need is differently interpreted: as due
to individual inadequacy or as a result of discrimination or systemic ills. A
focus on movement along a continuum misses varied perceptions of the
service-learning experience. Further, many preservice teachers seem
stalled in personal connections; they grasp life circumstances, problems,
and solutions through the lives of "needy" individuals. A continuum of
learning assumes more progress, especially more grasp of social problems
than might occur. Finally, concerns for justice often are construed as a call
for "better" teaching. These complications are lost in visions of progressive learning, as movement from one point of reference to another.

Multicultural service learning underscored multicultural education.
It afforded occasions to become acquainted with people different from
oneself, to situate children within family and community life, and to identify assets and resources within culturally diverse or economically distressed
neighborhoods. However, multicultural service learning, in the forms presented here, skirted issues of systemic inequality. Reflective sessions tended
to root out stereotypes, but leave social or institutional inequities alone.
As a result, the impact of life conditions on children's hopes and dreams
was misunderstood. As Ryan's reflection indicates, "trauma" at home is
vaguely grasped and secondary to the learning experience.

Some aspects of a broadly conceptualized multicultural education, as
outlined in Chapter 1, were supported, others were not. Multicultural
service learning affirmed cultural difference, especially as an aspect of

sound teaching. Multicultural service learning was antiracist, but more as alterations in preservice teacher's individual perspectives than as challenges to systemic racism. Multicultural service learning spurred thoughts of more equal and fair schooling and was especially helpful in redefining education as something that takes place in schools, homes, and communities. Multicultural service learning was critical pedagogy, especially in delving into local problems through reflective discussions. However, further systemic analysis was needed to situate real events in contexts of institutional or social inequality.

These findings indicate that prior life experience should be a factor of consideration in multicultural service learning. Placements should offer novel, cross-cultural experiences for preservice teachers. Culturally mixed service learning teams can enrich cross-cultural experiences by affording opportunities to learn from one's peers. Community instructors can serve as cultural brokers to communities, aiding preservice teachers in understanding contexts distinct from their own.

Paradigmatic orientations to issues of culture, race, and power should be addressed. Instructors should clarify their own stance and situate their aims for service learning paradigmatically. They should realize that service learners will pick up dispositions toward difference and equality advanced by social agencies and community organizations. If placed in a charitable association, service learners likely will glean a charitable stance. Mismatches between the aims for multicultural service learning and the character of service-learning sites should be addressed. Additionally, distinctions between paradigmatic stances should be taught in order to help preservice teachers locate their ideas and grasp their own conceptual development.

A broadly conceptualized multicultural education encompasses multiple dimensions, from cultural knowledge to systemic critique. Multicultural service learning with a range of diverse people lends itself to cultural and social awareness, acceptance, and affirmation. Institutional or social critique must be mounted apart from the experience. Real events can be utilized as a catalyst for critical social assessment. As a field experience for teacher education, social justice issues naturally are interpreted through the lens of teaching. However, preservice teachers need guidance to understand "becoming a better teacher" in broader terms than regard for individual learning differences. Teaching as advocacy for one's students might serve as a frame for critical contemplation of equal, excellent teaching.

Conceptual Framework

The conceptual framework proposed by Christine Sleeter and I (Boyle-Baise & Sleeter, 2000) was substantiated by this research. Preservice teachers, profiled in Chapter 3, held deficit or affirmative views of cultural diversity and poverty. Affirmative views ranged from liberal notions of equal status to budding ideas about social justice in schools. Pragmatic views, focused on becoming a better teacher, were articulated across the board, by all four of the preservice teachers profiled. Activist views were expressed only among preservice teachers of color and emphasized the school as a locus for social change.

The profiles of preservice teachers complicated this framework as well. Deficit views were not only a facet of white prospective teachers' views. Preservice teachers of color held biased views of white people as well. For both groups, multicultural service learning helped debunk stereotypes and disrupt faulty assumptions. During the course of service learning, all four preservice teachers gained increased ease in racially or ethnically mixed contexts. Initially, pragmatic views were identified as a separate stance for a few preservice teachers. In Chapter 3, all of the preservice teachers profiled articulated pragmatic concerns. Multicultural service learning was perceived as a prime opportunity to gain attitudes and practice skills to become a better teacher. Becoming a better teacher was perceived differently within this small group. Preservice teachers of color confronted issues of racial equality, multiple perspectives, and social integration more than their white counterparts. The meanings made by white preservice teachers located them solidly within the liberal camp or civic education paradigm. The perspectives of preservice teachers of color indicated that they were activists in the making, as teacher advocates for diverse youth. The willingness of a white preservice teacher to place himself in situations where he could learn from being in the minority suggested a route to activism for teachers from majority groups.

Based on this information, the debunking of deficit views should be a central task for multicultural service learning. However, it should not be an impetus interpreted only according to majority group positions. Instead, the reconsideration of stereotypes and assumptions needs to be subtler. It needs to account for variation in bias and misinformation among majority and minority cultural and social class groups. Many white preservice teachers are stalled in a "kids are all alike" and a "equal playing field" liberal stance. Both notions need to be problematized. One approach is to deal with dualism and resiliency in childrens' lives, how they can face adversity and still find moments of childhood happiness. Another strategy is to interrogate the shortcomings of the meritorious equal opportunity argument.

Becoming a better teacher is a fundamental reason for multicultural service learning. I expected preservice teachers to gain cultural knowledge and to question inequality as bases for change making in schools. Most white prospective teachers hoped to learn to handle diverse youngsters and to meet their needs through modified instructional strategies. Preservice teachers of color, in contrast, wrestled with impacts of culture and race on themselves and their future teaching in ways that correlated with my aims for the project. Frank discussion of expectations (and possible cross-purposes) could strengthen the experience. Significant concern with becoming a better teacher opens the door to consider its translation as part of a broadly conceptualized multicultural education.

Activism, in terms of antiracist or equitable teaching, is too faintly expressed for an endeavor in multicultural service learning. Preservice teachers tend to encounter and interpret multicultural service learning from where they are in terms of personal, cultural, and social background. At issue is how (and to what extent) one can dislodge a majority of preservice teachers from charitable or liberal orientations and engage them in social change views, especially given the short duration of multicultural service learning. It is a question that remains. As my journey continues, I plan to utilize preservice teachers' efforts to work through their own racism as a springboard for discussions of antiracist teaching. This conceptual framework, and the complications to it, serve as a clarification device. It alerts instructors to preservice teachers' perceptions and, in so doing, allows them to make informed decisions about practice.

Practices

When supervision of and tasks for service learning were left to the discretion of community liaisons, preservice teachers fit into prescribed volunteer roles. They tended to focus on and learn most about youth through one-on-one tutor or mentor situations. In contexts, like churches, where family attendance was characteristic, preservice teachers developed positive views of families, but still observed them from afar. These roles played it too safe for multicultural service learning.

In order to meet aims of a broadly conceptualized multicultural education, service learning needs to move beyond tutoring and passive observation. Preservice teachers need to view youth in capacities other than students, to interact intensively with families, to recognize community assets, and to grapple with community concerns. A task-based contract spoke to these aims. It set an array of tasks for service learning that disallowed a singular focus or passivity. In this case, the contract spoke to glaring omissions in multicultural service learning. While a work contract and a range of field tasks seemed worthwhile, the dimensions of the contract are not reified. Rather, the contract is an impetus early in its development. Binding agreements of varied types have potential for multicultural service learning.

I still struggle with activities that augment multicultural service learning. The recognition of community liaisons as coteachers was of immense benefit to the project. Preservice teachers and I gained insights into community affairs otherwise impossible to get. Additionally, teaching and learning was diversified by the multiple perspectives and life experiences of coteachers. Yet, functioning as a community of teachers was an extremely complicated endeavor, and it accorded such respect to partners that criticism of their programs was forestalled.

The mini-inquiry project met some aims, but stymied others. I stand by the need to learn to study communities in which one teaches. In order to provide a multicultural education, teachers need to understand students' learning outside school and link their teaching to it. I still believe it is critical to learn to probe questions of local import by speaking with those people to whom the query pertains. However, a full-blown field study might not be necessary to achieve these aims. A case study of a child or family might suffice. Further, reflective discussions tend to scratch the surface of cultural and racial issues. In the future, I do not intend to rely solely on this structure to promote systemic inquiry. My trials continue. Several criteria will guide my future construction of tasks for multicultural service learning: emphasis on youth as members of cultural groups and communities, examination of children's learning outside schools, linkage of home and school contexts, and recognition of local community assets.

LESSONS LEARNED: COMMUNITY PARTNERS

In Chapter 6, I described multicultural service learning as a nexus of relationships. It is an educational process carried out in the field, in partnership with representatives from culturally diverse and low-income communities. I noted also that it took time to construct these relationships. Possibly, shared control epitomizes a later stage in one's integration of multicultural education and service learning. In the following sections, I reiterate theory and practice involved in working with community partners to create and implement multicultural service learning.

Theories and Philosophies

"Working with" community liaisons as a community of teachers was posed as an affirmative approach to multicultural service learning. "Working with" stood for personal attachment, based on honest respect and earned trust among a small group of educational reformers. "Working with" symbolized a covenant of equal partnership, balanced in commitment and obligation. "Working with" represented an affirmation of diversity within a pluralistic university-community coalition. "Working with" rested on principles for quality service learning, for community building, and for multicultural education.

In order to demonstrate sound service learning, interrelations were characterized by reciprocity, mutuality, and power. Usually, discussions of balanced, mutually beneficial service learning stops short of considerations of power. In this case, shared, dispersed power was at the core of the community partnership. The university-community group functioned as a coalition of concerned citizens, intent on transforming one small moment in teacher education. The coalition aimed to empower community-based learning as an aspect of multicultural teacher education. In granting power to community learning, power was conferred on local people as community brokers, teachers, and guides.

In order to build community and to bolster multicultural education, common causes were developed, ideas were freely expressed, true dialogue was fostered, and passions of pluralism were demonstrated. It is artificial to separate impetuses for community building from passions for pluralism. As an exercise in multicultural education, appreciation for cultural diversity, plural ideas, equal status, and joint action were part and parcel of the coalition. Multicultural education framed this partnership; it established its tone, guided its interactions, and undergirded its activities. As the partners struggled with a common cause, community was constructed. Passions for pluralism—as face-to-face conversations among a culturally diverse group about issues of difference and power—identifies these struggles and captures their fervor.

In this partnership, shared control embodied all these principles. To share meant to be fully and equally engaged. It meant admitting a personal stake in the project. It meant making meaningful contributions and taking collective action. It meant alliance with people different from oneself. To control meant to have authority. It meant dispersing the power of teaching among the partners. It meant validating community folks as teachers and evaluators, and it meant empowering them personally as well. Control meant voicing one's values and views and practicing skills of supervision and instruction. The concept of a *community of teachers* might represent these purposes equally well and forego the negative connotations of control, held by at least one community partner.

Practices

Shared control was practiced through contractual promise. The task-based contract, simple and straightforward as it might seem, forged a commitment hitherto absent. It undergirded the partnership. Signed by the community partner and the preservice teacher, the task-based contract bound each to the other. It set clear expectations for service learning and included activities pertinent to a broadly conceptualized multicultural education. The contract also represented a larger agreement among the partners. We promised each other to hold up our end of the board, to provide feedback on essays, to attend reflective sessions, and to assist with the mini-inquiry. Promises made and kept set the tone for the partnership. The clarity of the contract steadied a diffuse, decentralized, multi-faceted teaching endeavor.

The six major tasks for service learning worked as a quid pro quo: Preservice teachers offered their time and served as an extra hand, and community partners created a learning space for them within local organizations. Prior to the effort to share control, service and learning were imbalanced, with more emphasis on service than on learning. Actually, a slight imbalance remained, this time tilted toward a learning experience for preservice teachers.

The tasks demonstrate one attempt to move beyond tutoring to heightened interaction with community instructors, youth, and families and to elevated attention to local issues. Chapter 6 sketches a trial run of the task-based set up. The trial highlighted imperfections and suggested modifications. These have been detailed elsewhere, so a summary will suffice.

The tasks were perceived as reasonable and doable. Community partners had little trouble, beyond the limits of personal time, in their supervision of tasks. Partners found it taxing to evaluate preservice teachers, especially without personal measures of commitment in assessment criteria. The logistics of dispersing, reading, and returning reflective essays was mind-boggling, yet the feedback thus rendered diversified the instruction preservice teachers received. Reflective discussions sometimes suffered from overly bland guiding questions and from limited social analysis, but both are resolved easily. Partners should be assisted in the development of questions to guide discussion, and subsequent class sessions should be devoted to social critique. Sleeter (1995) offers a useful framework for social and institutional analysis. She helps her students puzzle through social realities from dominant and minority *position* perspectives, a consideration of worldviews from different locations in the social order.

LEARNING LESSONS

This book is based upon two types of inquiry: interpretive-ethnographic and action research. For preservice teachers, I mounted inquiry *on*: They were subjects for descriptive investigation of their perceptions and actions related to multicultural service learning. For community partners, I did inquiry *with*: They were coresearchers and cosubjects for action inquiry related to our partnership and to processes of service learning. One could reasonably ask, Why utilize one form of research for one group and a different form for the other? Why not broaden ethnographic inquiry to include perceptions and actions of community partners? Why not engage preservice teachers in action research?

In this section, I submit that ethnographic inquiry provides rich description of preservice teachers' experiences, but strains to capture multisited complexity; that action research respects collaborative efforts with community representatives, but leaves community contexts unexplored; and that action research with preservice teachers offers a new avenue for service learning inquiry. First, I situate these claims in the current climate of research on service learning.

Current Research on Multicultural Service Learning

At the collegiate level, most investigations of service learning are quantitative, survey-based, and comparative (Batchelder & Root, 1994; Giles & Eyler, 1994; Markus, Howard, & King, 1993; J. Miller, 1997; Osborne, Hammerich, & Hensley, 1998; Vadeboncoeur et al., 1996). Often, survey data, course evaluations, and final grades are collected from course sections with a service-learning component and compared to sections without one. Most of this research focuses on impacts for participants, meaning college students (Wutzdorff & Giles, 1997). Commonly, surveys measure the attainment of goals for individual learning: personal growth, grasp of subject matter, and development of citizenship values and skills (Giles, Honnet, & Migliore, 1991). Eyler and Giles' (1999) research, based on a national database of over 1,500 college students, is a capstone of this approach. The pre/post orientation of this research glosses over what actually happens within service learning.

A small body of qualitative research yields information about service learning as a dimension of multicultural education, social foundations, or child development courses. In these studies, service learning is located in culturally diverse or low-income situations. Similar to the quantitative inquiries, this research focuses on impacts of service learning upon preservice teachers. Some research anecdotally describes preservice teachers' field activities and impressions thereof (Sleeter, 1995; Tellez et al., 1995). Other studies focus on meaning making among preservice teachers, based on their reflective writings (Dunlap, 1998; O'Grady & Chappell, 2000) and, to a lesser extent, on their interviews as well (Boyle-Baise, 1998; Fuller, 1998;

Hones, 1997). In most studies, respondents are white, but a few studies also sample preservice teachers of color (Boyle-Baise & Efiom, 2000; Boyle-Baise & Sleeter, 2000). This literature offers a detailed portrait of preservice teachers' impressions of multicultural service learning.

Few studies offer field-based reconstructions of multicultural service learning. Chapter 4 addresses this need and exemplifies on-site description of what really happens during service learning. Beth Chappell (O'Grady & Chappell, 2000) describes her own service-learning experiences as a tutor in an English-as-a-second-language classroom. Her description is a rare example of action research by a preservice teacher.

The community as a dimension of service learning mostly is over-looked in research. As noted in Chapter 5, Cruz and Giles (2000) find the lack of research on community dimensions of service learning a "glaring omission" (p. 28). They suggest a collaborative, action research approach to studying service-learning partnerships.

Issues for Research on Multicultural Service Learning

Although not usually directed toward multicultural education, there is plenty of survey research that suggests positive affective and academic outcomes of service learning for college students. For multicultural service learning, more investigation of meaning making among preservice teachers is needed, especially inclusive of future teachers of color. More description of preservice teachers in action, doing community-based service learning, also is needed. More studies of community engagement in service learning are urgently wanted. I raise issues in regard to these needs based on my own service-learning research. I speak to three issues particularly: holism, collaboration, and representation.

Holism. What does it mean to holistically depict a multi-sited service-learning experience? Who should be included in holistic descriptions? Is it necessary to capture it all?

There are bonafide reasons to study what preservice teachers think about service learning and what happens during their field experiences. Teacher educators, in particular, seek to understand the impact of community-based service learning as a dimension of multicultural education. Preservice teachers, fortunately, are ready research informants. They attend education classes regularly, part and parcel of the university as a research institution. If provided with adequate safeguards for their privacy or their course grades, prospective teachers usually are an amenable research pool.

Community representatives, alternatively, pose problems for research. For adults, there is no reason, beyond the immediate bounds of a study, to probe their lives. If community partners' lives outside the study are held sacrosanct, then many personal views, possibly related to the study, remain unknown. Culture, power, and privilege differences between researchers and community liaisons complicate inquiry further. Doing research in disenfranchised communities, where most service learning takes place, is a sensitive effort in human relations.

Investigation of youth is terribly problematic. Underage individuals need stringent protection from possible detriments of research. The provision of a secure research environment for youth is difficult by any standards, but it is complicated by fluidity, uncertainty, and multiplicity in service learning. Community centers, for example, have fluid, drop-in populations—in attendance one day, absent the next. It is difficult to identify a stable population from whom to seek permission for research.

Multicultural service learning tends to be multisituated. Neighborhood associations and churches, often the best sites for local acuity and affirmative orientations, usually are too small to mentor large groups of preservice teachers. Four to six sites always have been necessary to my work with multicultural service learning. Moreover, preservice teachers volunteer at different hours, attend varied functions, and complete diverse tasks, all under the supervision of individual community partners. Holistic description easily becomes overwhelming. It is no wonder that survey research of college students close at hand seems the method of choice for inquiry on service learning.

The following account, focused only on preservice teachers, exemplifies the complexities of multisituated inquiry. During the fall of 1998, my research assistant, Jim Kilbane, observed six inquiry teams at least four times each, for about 2 hours each time, from Monday through Sunday, in churches and in after-school programs. Jim stayed through a session of activity, but activities often were brief. For example, Girl Scout meetings were over in an hour or so. We gathered a number of well-focused snapshots of service-learning activities across the board. However, we did not study any one site with duration and depth.

All social contexts are characterized by complexity and multiplicity. Events occur simultaneously, and groups engage in different activities at the same time. Mobility complicates matters. Researchers struggle to be present in multiple sites. In so doing, Jim and I felt that something significant slipped our grasp. Arguably, what we lost in depth, we gained in breadth. We gleaned information that allowed us to study similarity and difference across sites.

An alternative to a broad approach is a focus on one or two sites, as representative of a service-learning effort. Subsequent to the study above, another research assistant, Susan Johnstad, helped me investigate two service-learning sites, deemed promising from the earlier inquiry. Both organizations served the same neighborhood, enjoyed local leaders, and were viewed positively by preservice teachers. We probed similarities and differences between these sites. We balanced our previous snapshots of activities with sustained study. Yet, the synthesis of these two studies is problematic inasmuch as it mixes inquiries from different moments in time. The selection of two sites from among many also raises questions of representation.

These studies, though elaborate, underplayed community dimensions: community liaisons were secondary informants and youth participants were sidestepped carefully. Yet, a focus on one group, preservice teachers, narrowed inquiry to workable proportions. George Marcus (1995/1998) suggests a viable focus for multisituated, ethnographic accounts. He redefines holism from extensive cultural description of one site to illumination of cultural phenomena across sites. Marcus advises investigators to "follow the people, thing, metaphor, or story" (pp. 90–93) across research sites. For multicultural service learning, researchers might follow the preservice teachers, or the development of cross-cultural relationships, or the process of becoming a multicultural teacher. A phenomenological emphasis affords comparison of the thing or process across sites. For example, in Chapter 4, a comparison of service-learning activities across sites showed preservice teachers commonly operated within predetermined volunteer roles.

Of course, an impressive team of researchers or, at least, a full-time lone investigator might grapple with holism in its fullest sense—across locales and within them. The pursuit of research funds to gain time to concentrate on research or to support full-time researchers should not be cast aside.

Collaboration. How do aims for mutual regard impact research on multicultural service learning? What does it mean to include community partners in inquiry? Can preservice teachers collaborate in service-learning investigations?

Early in this journey, I focused on the construction of authentic, nuanced expressions of preservice teachers' attitudes, values, and views. My community associates remained at the margins of my research. They granted permission to study their sites, as long as it focused on preservice teachers rather than on themselves or their clientele. After semester's end, I met with my associates; we revisited our aims, reviewed our ends, and considered future emphases. Later, I sent my associates a brief research update that described preservice teachers' perceptions of cultural diversity, racism, and poverty, at least partly influenced by service learning within their organizations. Community collaboration, at this time, meant minimal inclusion in plans for and reassessment of multicultural service learning.

Upon receipt of one of my research updates, two community representatives, both locally active women of color, invited me to lunch. They were startled by false presumptions about race and poverty among preservice teachers, yet heartened by possibilities of multicultural service learning. They offered their assistance as mentors to the multicultural education class. One of the women subsequently joined reflective class discussions and offered her impressions of service-learning experiences. As I transcribed videotapes of these reflective sessions, I heard a substantially different, insider outlook on issues of difference and equality. Afterward, I invited the community mentor to participate in writing a chapter with me. We decided to write a multivocal text in which we identified our own voices and views in different sections of the chapter (Boyle-Baise & Efiom, 2000). These experiences alerted me to the richness of working with community representatives as coplanners, coteachers, and coauthors.

About the same time, I turned my attention to the dearth of on-site observational data in my queries. I conducted the study that underpins Chapter 4. I still focused on preservice teachers, but interviewed community associates as an ongoing part of the inquiry. After the investigation, I shared a paper derived from the research with my community associates. Most were intrigued by the findings, but a few hoped for an even stronger presence in the research. Additionally, I felt my voice was muted, in order to distance myself as instructor from an experience in which I was a part. We decided to intensify our work together and to jointly write a research paper which conveyed our experiences as full project participants.

For this next endeavor, the term partnership took on new meaning. We cooperated from start to finish to plan, implement, and evaluate a cycle of multicultural service learning. We inquired into our own perceptions and actions via two "research forums." The forums form the basis for Chapter 5. I have not collaborated with preservice teachers similarly. Of course, preservice teachers participate in research by allowing me to include their data in my inquiries. Yet, this approach does not treat them as coresearchers. I can imagine working with a small group of preservice teachers who volunteer to study themselves in action, doing and making meaning of multicultural service learning. The group might plan, discuss, and debate their actions related to service learning, comparable to the self-study undertaken by the community partnership. The engagement of preservice teachers directly in research is a remaining challenge.

Representation. Whose voices should be heard in descriptions of this endeavor? What might preservice teachers have to say, if offered a format in which to "speak?" How should the perspectives of community partners be included?

As a companion to a broadly conceptualized multicultural education, service learning is a vehicle for interaction with and learning from disenfranchised communities. In this case, working with people of color or low-income communities has been the focus. The metaphor of "border crossing" (Giroux, 1992) is pertinent to the crisscross of life experiences that occurs within multicultural service learning. Crossing borders does not simply imply that white teachers enter communities of color, although they do. Recall Natalie's experience (in Chapter 3). She is an African American preservice teacher who, when welcomed into a racially mixed church, developed greater ease in cross-race situations. As a dimension of multicultural service learning and thus as a factor in its research, border crossing encourages examination of cultural or social boundaries and of cross-group relations. For example, my community partners offer perspectives from different cultural and social standpoints. Attention to border crossing brings questions of difference to the forefront in relation to issues of representation.

In Chapter 5, I submitted that the community partnership within which I worked was a representative slice from a geographic and cultural community. A claim like this is open to question. Our actual representativeness is not the point. I want to argue that border crossing, as a factor for multicultural service learning, obliged my attention to difference and power in the selection of research partners, in the choice of inquiry method, and in the configuration of the research report. It might organize further service-learning research in this manner.

As mentioned earlier, when I explained the partners' participation in collective inquiry to my multicultural education class, a small group of prospective teachers volunteered to contemplate, then write about their own views. A plausible format for the incorporation of preservice teachers' thoughts and actions on their own terms had presented itself. Commentary from a small cooperative study group can admit unmitigated standpoints of preservice teachers into service-learning research. Although a collaborative group did not form from that conversation, Ryan's reflections stem from it.

Issues of representation also are issues of presentation. How should we portray different voices in our texts? Authors have used a multivoiced text (e.g., Lather & Smithies, 1997), and although a bit awkward to read, this device clearly acknowledges joint efforts. My highlight of quotations from community partners and inclusion of reflective interludes are editorial inventions to diversify and personalize voice. Additionally, coauthorship, such as the joint effort with my community partners in Chapter 5, challenges the dominion of a sole researcher and broadens representation.

Issues of representation also are issues of interpretation. The same context can be interpreted differently by separate observers. A rendering is, in the end result, the author's own. As my ethical responsibility, I shared drafts of chapters with respondents and coauthors and solicited their revisions. However, I constructed the draft and, in so doing, set the framework for their review. In other words, I drew the box, and my informants and colleagues functioned inside it. Collaborative action inquiry affords opportunities to research outside the box, inviting interpretations divergent from one's own. The quest is to develop forms which showcase multiple interpretations. I suggested that the partners keep journals, then utilize our entries to write reflective segments, like the bridges or interludes between chapters. However, we did not act on this idea. Questions about courting diverse interpretations remain.

RESEARCH DIRECTIONS FOR MULTICULTURAL SERVICE LEARNING

The recommendations that follow derive from lessons learned, from general needs for service-learning research, and from investigative issues raised in my work. I speak first to inquiry centered on preservice teachers, second to research with community partners, and third to an aggregate of both.

It is important to know what meanings preservice teachers make from multicultural service learning. Relevant questions might be asked: Does multicultural service learning disrupt cultural and racial stereotypes and forestall denigration? Does it promote cross-cultural understanding? Does it jar notions of privilege? Does it propel future teachers toward change making in schools? Future interpretive studies can substantiate, clarify, and critique the conceptual framework and paradigmatic views posed here. Such studies raise other pertinent questions: What paradigmatic views do preservice teachers hold? What conceptual shifts, if any, are articulated by preservice teachers? Investigations should include perspectives from a diverse range of preservice teachers.

More field studies are needed that go beyond surveys, impressions, and anecdotal evidence to learn what really happens inside multicultural service learning. In order to grapple with multisituated research, a phenomenological approach seems reasonable. Investigators follow the people, thing, metaphor, or story across sites. A focus on preservice teachers has integrity, but should benefit from more community context than I often provided. Relevant questions for descriptive studies would provide that context: What paradigmatic position does the community organization take on cultural diversity and poverty? Who leads the association, what are his or her views on diversity, equality, and excellent education, and how does his or her supervision impact preservice teachers? What kinds of cross-cultural interactions do preservice teachers have with youth and families inside different community associations? What occurrences serve to disrupt preservice teacher's assumptions and biases; what happened and how was it interpreted?

The inclusion of preservice teachers as cosubjects and coresearchers through action research formats deserves trial and study. A representative subgroup of preservice teachers might write action/reflection essays, then collaboratively puzzle through trends and disparities in their thoughts and actions. Doing research *with*, not *on*, preservice teachers potentially yields another voice and view for service-learning research.

The notion of *working with* community representatives as full partners, for teaching and for inquiry, demands more study. Two formats were described here: cooperative experiential inquiry (action research) and the development of multivocal texts. Action research, as a vehicle that respects collaboration and responds to the dynamic character of service learning, needs more trial and consideration. Metaphors of shared control and border crossing were offered as guides to the construction and research of collaborative efforts. A task-based contract was described as one mode of collaboration. Questions to raise about community participation in research include the following: What does it mean to "work with" community liaisons? What does it mean to "share control" with community partners? How, if at all, does border crossing serve as a criterion for inquiry? Relatedly, to what extent does a task-based contract sustain community partnership?

George Marcus (1989/1998) prods investigators to say more about contexts of descriptive field studies than is the traditional case. He outlines four strategies to do so: (1) Say more by letting others say it; (2) say more by juxtaposing multiple levels and styles of analysis; (3) say more through critique of dominant forms of thought; and (4) say more by saying it all. Collaborative action research especially speaks to strategies one and four. More can be said about multicultural service learning when university researchers let others say it. For multicultural service learning, the "others who say it" need to represent a range of cultural and social diversity. A multiplistic cadre is more likely to put forth diverse interpretations. A research study might say more through the development of a corps of action researchers; both community representatives and preservice teachers can be included in this team.

Can researchers say more by saying it all? There are fundamental differences between descriptive, ethnographic approaches and action research (Longstreet, 1982). Ethnographers usually study contexts from afar, as detached observers. Action researchers commonly study contexts from within, as involved participants. The two formats cannot be mixed without great care. However, they can form the basis for a mixed investigative approach. I can envision a collaborative inquiry group of preservice teachers meeting and reflecting amidst a larger, descriptive field study. I can anticipate simultaneous action inquiries by preservice teachers and community partners. The complexity of the research approach is limited more by an investigator's wherewithal to sustain it than by incongruous inquiry stances.

This book is based on a personal journey highly informed by ongoing research. I learned from my research, altered my subsequent practice, and grappled with new puzzlements as they arose. The book offers a firm research basis for further inquiry into multicultural service learning. I still wonder why, how, and in what ways community-based learning, as service learning, can supplement multicultural education for preservice teachers. My journey of inquiry and practice continues. I hope the questions raised by this research intrigue others and initiate similar journeys.

Case Study Methodology

Sample

Twenty-four preservice teachers comprised the case. Twenty preservice teachers were white: 7 males and 13 females. Four women were of color: 2 Latinas and 2 African Americans. According to a demographic survey, all but 2 preservice teachers were in-state students, most from small or middle-size towns. Most described their neighborhoods as middle-income, but 5 were from high-income and 3 were from low-income backgrounds. Most preservice teachers had minimal direct experience with cultural diversity or poverty, but several had traveled internationally with the armed forces, and a few others had worked in summer camps for low-income youth or for children with disabilities.

Data Collection

Jim Kilbane was a participant-observer and collected the data. I was a complete participant and taught the multicultural course (R. L. Gold, cited in LeCompte & Preissle, 1993). My participation in the research was disclosed fully, but was perceived as secondary to my teaching role. We met weekly to discuss what was happening in the field and in the class. We shared what we saw in our roles as participant and participant observer and developed questions for small-group interviews.

Kilbane observed each site from 4 to 12 times, depending upon the number of inquiry teams placed there. Overall, 33 site visits were made. Field notes were taken and an observation schedule was used. Observations lasted 1 to 3 hours, contingent upon the activities underway. Kilbane stayed until a cycle of activities was completed and until he got a feel for the repetitive nature of what happened.

Preservice teachers were interviewed as site-based teams three times, at the beginning, middle, and end of community service learning. Organization directors were interviewed after the service experience. Reflective sessions were audiotaped and field notes were taken during discussions. Also, written assignments were included in our data base.

Data Analysis

We studied multiple forms of data (e.g., interviews, observations, and reflective essays) from varied sources (i.e., preservice teachers, organization directors). Reference to varied sources triangulated our interpretations. Interviews and reflective essays were read to determine recurrent ideographic themes (Spindler & Spindler, 1997). If an idea was reiterated by several respondents, it was considered influential (Youniss & Yates, 1997). Constant comparison analysis (Glaser & Strauss, 1967) was used to search for diversity within reflective papers and discussions. Attention was paid to site-based differences and to influences of race and gender. For observation data, we searched for repeated forms of and reasons behind behavior, then we contrasted norms with critical incidents that stood apart as unusual.

We read the data separately, then cross-checked our interpretations. For the most part, we identified similar trends. When we differed, we rechecked the data. Usually, from our alternate standpoints, one of us saw or heard something the other did not, and we were able to amplify our categorizations. Most puzzling were differences between preservice teachers' expressions of serious self-assessment and seemingly limited field activities. This potential disjuncture became a focal point for our deliberations.

Limitations

As I was the course instructor, issues of power might have influenced the investigation. Care was taken to reduce potential feelings of coercion. As instructor, I did not interview or observe respondents. Preservice teachers could opt out of the study after the assignment of grades for the course, although none did. Names were used on reflective essays, and frankness could have been impacted. For this reason, essays were counted as completed assignments, but not graded.

Questions Guiding
Research Forums

Forum One: September 8, 1999

- Why did you decide to participate in this project?
- What does the idea of *shared control* for community-based service learning mean to you?
- What has it been like for you to participate in planning this project?
- How, if at all, do you think both parties, teacher education and your organization, will benefit from this service learning arrangement?
- What, if anything, do you find most promising or problematic about this partnership?
- What would you like to add that has not been asked?

Forum Two: December 10, 1999

- Generally, what did partnership in this project mean for you?
- What did you think about the task-based contracts? Were they a good learning tool? If yes, why? If no, why not?
- What was it like for you to evaluate your team?
- Did this level of participation expect too much? too little? about right?
- Has this project affected you personally in any way?
- What would you like to add that has not been asked?

APPENDIX C

Evaluation Criteria

Grading

C+: Satisfactory quality of work—completes at least 75% of service hours (15) and task contract, but attends irregularly or participates minimally

B: Very good, solid, above average quality of work—completes all hours and assignments, is a solid member of the inquiry team

A: Extraordinarily high achievement; high degree of originality or creativity—completes all hours and assignments and adds special leadership or creativity to projects

139

References

Ashton, P., & Webb, R. (1986). *Making a difference: Teacher's sense of efficacy and student achievement*. New York: Longman.

Au, K., & Kawakami, A. (1991). Culture and ownership: Schooling of minority students. *Childhood Education, 67*(5), 280–284.

Banks, J. (1988). *Multiethnic education: Theory and practice* (2nd ed.). Boston: Allyn & Bacon.

Banks, J. A. (1995). Multicultural education: Historical development, dimensions, and practice. In J. A. Banks & C. M. Banks (Eds.), *Handbook of research on multicultural education* (pp. 3–24). New York: MacMillan.

Banks, J. (2001). Multicultural education: Characteristics and goals. In J. Banks & C. McGee Banks (Eds.), *Multicultural education: Issues and perspectives* (pp. 3–30). New York: John Wiley & Sons.

Barber, B. (1992). *An aristocracy of everyone: The politics of education and the future of America*. New York: Oxford University Press.

Barber, B. (1998). *A passion for democracy: American essays*. Princeton, NJ: Princeton University Press.

Batchelder, T., & Root, S. (1994). Effects of an undergraduate program to integrate academic learning and service: Cognitive, prosocial cognitive, and identity outcomes. *Journal of Adolescence, 17*(4), 341–345.

Battsioni, R. (2000). Service learning and civic education. In S. Mann & J. Patrick (Eds.), *Education for civic engagement in democracy* (pp. 29–44). Bloomington, IN: ERIC Clearinghouse for Social Studies/Social Science Education.

Bennett, C. I. (1999). *Comprehensive multicultural education: Theory and practice* (4th ed.). Boston: Allyn & Bacon.

Boyle-Baise, M. (1998). Community service learning for multicultural education: An exploratory study with preservice teachers. *Equity and Excellence in Education, 31*(2), 52–60.

Boyle-Baise, M. (1999, Summer). "As good as it gets?" The impact of philosophical orientations on community-based service learning for multicultural education. *The Educational Forum, 63*, 310–320.

Boyle-Baise, M.,& Efiom, P. (2000). The construction of meaning: Learning from service learning. In C. O'Grady (Ed.), *Integrating service learning and multicultural education in colleges and universities* (pp. 209–226). Mahwah, NJ: Erlbaum.

Boyle-Baise, M., & Kilbane, J. (2000). What really happens? A look inside service learning for multicultural teacher education. *Michigan Journal of Community Service Learning, 7*, 54–64.

Boyle-Baise, M., & Sleeter, C. E. (2000). Community-based service learning for multicultural teacher education. *Educational Foundations, 14*(2), 33–50.

Bringle, R., & Hatcher, J. (1996). Implementing service learning in higher education. *Journal of Higher Education, 67*(2), 221–239.

Chesler, M. (1995). Service, service-learning, and change-making. In J. Galura, J. Howard, D. Waterhouse, & R. Ross (Eds.), *Praxis III: Voices in dialogue* (pp. 137–141). Ann Arbor, MI: OCSL Press.

Chesler, M., & Scalera, C. (2000). Race and gender issues related to service-learning research. *Michigan Journal of Community Service Learning*, (special issue), 18–27.

Cruz, N., & Giles, D. (2000). Where's the community in service-learning research? *Michigan Journal of Community Service Learning*, (Special Issue), 28–33.

Delgado-Gaitan, C. (1990). *Literacy for empowerment*. London: Falmer.

Delpit, L. (1995). *Other people's children: Cultural conflict in the classroom*. New York: The New Press.

Dewey, J. (1966). *Democracy and education*. New York: Free Press. (Original work published 1916)

Dunlap, M. (1998). Voices of students in multicultural service-learning settings. *Michigan Journal of Community Service Learning, 5,* 58–67.

Ehrlich, T. (1997, Summer). Civic learning: Democracy and education revisited. *Educational Record, 78*(3–4), 57–65.

Eisner, E. (1985). *The educational imagination: On the design and evaluation of school programs*. New York: Macmillan.

Eyler, J., & Giles, D. (1999). *Where's the learning in service-learning?* San Francisco: Jossey-Bass.

Festenstein, M. (1997). *Pragmatism & political theory: From Dewey to Rorty*. Chicago: University of Chicago Press.

Flake, F. (1999). *The way of the bootstrapper: Nine action steps for achieving your dreams*. San Francisco: Harper.

Ford, M. (1979). *The development of an instrument for assessing levels of ethnicity in public school teachers*. Unpublished doctoral dissertation, University of Houston, Houston, TX.

Fuller, M. (1998, April). *Introducing multicultural preservice teachers to diversity through field experiences*. Paper presented at the annual meeting of the American Educational Research Association, San Diego, CA.

Furco, A. (1996). Service-learning: A balanced approach to experiential education. In Corporation for National Service (Ed.), *Expanding boundaries: Serving and Learning* (Vol. 1, pp. 2–6). Columbia, MD: Cooperative Education Association.

Gabelnick, F. (1997). Educating a committed citizenry. *Change, 29*(1), 30–35.

Gay, G. (1994). *At the essence of learning: Multicultural education*. West Lafayette, IN: Kappa Delta Phi.

Gay, G. (1995). Mirror images on common issues: Parallels between multicultural education and critical pedagogy. In C. E. Sleeter & P. McLaren (Eds.), *Multicultural education, critical pedagogy, and the politics of difference* (pp. 155–189). Albany: State University of New York Press.

Gelmon, S., Holland, B., Sarena, D., Seifer, S., Shinnamon, A., & Connors, K. (1998). Community-university partnerships for mutual learning. *Michigan Journal of Community Service Learning, 5,* 97–107.

Giles, D., & Eyler, J. (1994). The impact of a college community service labora-
tory on students' personal, social, and cognitive outcomes. *Journal of Adolescence, 17*(4), 327–339.

Giles, D., Honnet, E., & Migliore, S. (1991). *Research agenda for combining service
and learning in the 1990's*. Raleigh, NC: National Society for Internships and
Experiential Education.

Gillette, M., & Boyle-Baise, M. (1996). Multicultural education at the graduate
level. Assisting teachers in gaining multicultural understandings. *Theory and
Research in Social Education, 24*(3), 273–293.

Giroux, H. (1992). *Border crossings: Cultural workers and the politics of education*. New
York: Routledge.

Glaser, B., & Strauss, A. (1967). *The discovery of grounded theory: Strategies for qualitative research*. Chicago: Aldine.

Greene, M. (1988). *The dialectic of freedom*. New York: Teachers College Press.

Greene, M. (1993). The passions of pluralism: Multiculturalism and the expanding community. *Educational Researcher, 22*(1), 13–18.

Harding, S. (1991). *Whose science? Whose knowledge? Thinking from women's lives*.
Ithaca, NY: Cornell University Press.

Harper, N. (1999). *Urban churches, vital signs: Beyond charity toward justice*. Grand
Rapids, MI: W. B. Eerdmans.

Hollins, E. (1996). *Culture in school learning: Revealing the deep meaning*. Mahwah,
NJ: Erlbaum.

Hones, D. (1997, March). *Preparing teachers for diversity: A service-learning approach*.
Paper presented at the annual meeting for the American Educational Research Association, Chicago.

Kahne, J., & Westheimer, J. (1996). In the service of what? The politics of service
learning. *Phi Delta Kappan, 77*(9), 593–599.

Kotlowitz, A. (1991). *There are no children here: The story of two boys growing up in
the other America*. New York: Doubleday.

Kozol, J. (2000). *Ordinary resurrections: Children in the years of hope*. New York: Crown.

Kretzman, J., & McKnight, J. (1993). *Building communities from the inside out: A path
toward finding and mobilizing a community's assets*. Chicago: ACTA Publications.

Lather, P., & Smithies, C. (1997). *Troubling the angels: Women living with HIV/AIDS*.
Boulder, CO: Westview Press.

LeCompte, M., & Preissle, J. (1993). *Ethnography and qualitative design in educational research* (2nd ed.). New York: Academic Press.

LeSourd, S. (1997). Community service in a multicultural nation. *Theory Into Practice, 36*(3), 157–163.

Longstreet, W. (1982, Winter). Action research: A paradigm. *The Educational Forum,
46*(2), 135–158.

Mahan, J., Fortney, M., & Garcia, J. (1983). Linking the community to teacher
education: Toward a more analytical approach. *Action in Teacher Education,
5*(1/2), 1–10.

Marcus, G. (1998). Imagining the whole: Ethnography's contemporary efforts to
situate itself. In *Ethnography through thick and thin* (pp. 33–56). Princeton, NJ:
Princeton University Press. (Article originally published 1989)

Marcus, G. (1998). Ethnography in/of the world system: The emergence of multi-sited ethnography. In *Ethnography through thick and thin* (pp. 79–104). Princeton, NJ: Princeton University Press. (Article originally published 1995)

Markus, G., Howard, J., & King, D. (1993). Integrating community service and classroom instruction enhances learning: Results from an experiment. *Educational Evaluation and Policy Analysis, 15*(4), 410–419.

Miller, B. A. (1997). Service-learning in support of rural community development. In A. Waterman (Ed.), *Service-learning: Applications from the research* (pp. 107–125). Mahwah, NJ: Erlbaum.

Miller, J. (1997). The impact of service-learning experiences on students' sense of power. *Michigan Journal of Community Service Learning, 4,* 16–21.

Moll, L. (1992). Bilingual classroom studies and community analysis. *Educational Researcher, 21*(2), 20–24.

Moll, L., Amanti, C., Neff, D., & Gonzalez, N. (1992). Funds of knowledge for teaching: Using a qualitative approach to connect homes and classrooms. *Theory Into Practice, 31*(2), 132–140.

Morton, K. (1995). The irony of service: Charity, project and social change in service-learning. *Michigan Journal of Community Service Learning, 2,* 19–32.

Nieto, S. (1995). From brown heroes and holidays to assimilationist agendas: Reconsidering the critiques of multicultural education. In C. E. Sleeter & P. McLaren (Eds.), *Multicultural education, critical pedagogy, and the politics of difference* (pp. 191–220). Albany: State University of New York Press.

Nieto, S. (2000). *Affirming diversity: The sociopolitical context of multicultural education* (3rd ed.). New York: Longman.

O'Grady, C. (1997, March). *Service learning, educational reform, and the preparation of teachers: Program models and institutions.* Paper presented at the annual meeting of the American Educational Research Association, Chicago.

O'Grady, C. (Ed.). (2000). *Integrating service learning and multicultural education in colleges and universities.* Mahwah, NJ: Erlbaum.

O'Grady, C., & Chappell, B. (2000). With, not for: The politics of service learning in multicultural communities. In C. Ovando & P. McLaren (Eds.), *The politics of multiculturalism: Teachers and students in the cross-fire* (pp. 209–224). Boston: McGraw-Hill.

Osborne, R., Hammerich, S., & Hensley, C. (1998). Student effects of service-learning: Tracking change across a semester. *Michigan Journal of Community Service Learning, 5,* 5–13.

Radest, H. (1993). *Community service: Encounter with strangers.* Westport, CT: Praeger.

Rawls, J. (1971). *A theory of justice.* Cambridge, MA: Harvard University Press.

Reason, P. (1994). Three approaches to participative inquiry. In N. Denzin & Y. Lincoln (Eds.), *Handbook of qualitative research* (pp. 324–339). Thousand Oaks, CA: Sage.

Reason, P., & Heron, J. (1986). Research with people: The paradigm of cooperative experiential inquiry. *Person-centered Review, 1*(4), 456–476.

Rhoads, R. (1997). *Community service and higher learning: Explorations of the caring self.* Albany: State University of New York Press.

Rosenberger, C. (2000). Beyond empathy: Developing critical consciousness through service learning. In C. O'Grady (Ed.), *Integrating service learning and multicultural education in colleges and universities* (pp. 23–43). Mahwah, NJ: Erlbaum.

Sigmon, R. (1994). *Serving to learn, learning to serve*. Washington, DC: Council of Independent Colleges.

Sleeter, C. E. (1995). Reflections on my use of multicultural and critical pedagogy when students are White. In C. E. Sleeter & P. McLaren (Eds.), *Multicultural education, critical pedagogy, and the politics of difference* (pp. 413–437). Albany: State University of New York Press.

Sleeter, C. E. (1996). *Multicultural education as social activism*. Albany: State University of New York Press.

Sleeter, C. E. (2000). Strengthening multicultural education with community-based service learning. In C. O'Grady (Ed.), *Integrating service learning and multicultural education in colleges and universities* (pp. 263–276). Mahwah, NJ: Erlbaum.

Sleeter, C. E., & Grant, C. (1999). *Making choices for multicultural education* (3rd ed.). Columbus, OH: Merrill.

Spindler, G., & Spindler, L. (1997). Cultural process and ethnography: An anthropological perspective. In G. Spindler (Ed.), *Education and cultural process: Anthropological approaches* (pp. 56–76). Prospect Heights, IL: Waveland Press.

Strauss, A., & Corbin, J. (1994). Grounded theory methodology: An overview. In N. Denzin & Y. Lincoln (Eds.), *Handbook of qualitative research* (pp. 273–285). Thousand Oaks, CA: Sage.

Tellez, K., Hlebowitsh, P. S., Cohen, M., & Norwood, P. (1995). Social service field experiences and teacher education. In J. M. Larkin & C. E. Sleeter (Eds.), *Developing multicultural teacher education curricula* (pp. 65–78). Albany: State University of New York Press.

U.S. Department of Education, National Center for Education Statistics. (1997). *Minorities in higher education*. Washington, DC: U.S. Department of Education.

Vadeboncoeur, J., Rahm, J., Aguilera, D., & LeCompte, M. D. (1996). Building democratic character through community experiences in teacher education. *Education and Urban Society, 28*(2), 189–207.

Varlotta, L. (1997). Confronting consensus: Investigating the philosophies that have informed service learning's communities. *Educational Theory, 47*(4), 453–476.

Vernon, A., & Ward, K. (1999). Campus and community partnerships: Assessing impacts and strengthening connections. *Michigan Journal of Community Service Learning, 6,* 30–37.

Wade, R. (1998, November). *Service-learning in multicultural education: A review of the literature*. Paper presented at the annual meeting of the National Council for the Social Studies, Anaheim, CA.

Wade, R., & Yarbrough, D. (1997). Community service learning in student teaching: Toward the development of an active citizenry. *Michigan Journal of Community Service Learning, 4,* 42–55.

Woodson, R. (1998). *The triumphs of Joseph: How today's community healers are reviving our streets and neighborhoods*. New York: Free Press.

Wutzdorff, A., & Giles, D. (1997). Service learning in higher education. In J. Schine (Ed.), *Service learning* (96th yearbook of the National Society for the Study of Education, pp. 105–117). Chicago: National Society for the Study of Education.

Youniss, J., & Yates, M. (1997). *Community service and social responsibility in youth.* Chicago: University of Chicago Press.

Zeichner, K. (1992). Rethinking the practicum in the professional development school partnership. *Journal of Teacher Education, 43*(4), 296–307.

Zeichner, K. (1993). *Educating teachers for cultural diversity.* East Lansing, MI: National Center for Research on Teacher Learning.

Zeichner, K., & Melnick, S. (1996). The role of community field experiences in preparing teachers for cultural diversity. In. K. Zeichner, S. Melnick, & M. L. Gomez (Eds.), *Currents of reform in preservice teacher education* (pp. 176–196). New York: Teachers College Press.

Index

About the Authors

Lynne Boyle-Baise is an associate professor in Curriculum and Instruction at Indiana University, Bloomington (IUB). She teaches Curriculum Studies, Social Studies, and Multicultural Education and coordinates the Social Studies Program at IUB. She has written widely on multicultural education, social studies, and community service learning. Presently, she is investigating the impact of Alternative Spring Break, a community-based service-learning opportunity, on citizenship education.

Dr. Boyle-Baise is past chair of the College and University Faculty Assembly (CUFA) for the National Council of the Social Studies (NCSS). She serves on the board of Funds for the Advancement of Social Education (FASSE), a governance group within NCSS. She also serves on the Editorial Board of the *International Social Studies Forum* and has served on the Editorial Board of *Theory and Research in Social Education.*

Dr. Boyle-Baise lives in Bloomington, Indiana with her husband, Michael, and her Portugese water dog, DoMarco's Boston Tea Party. In spare moments, she enjoys walking, boating, and golfing.

The coauthor for Chapter 4, **Jim Kilbane**, is a doctoral student in Curriculum and Instruction at Indiana University. His dissertation is focused on ecological approaches to schooling.

Coauthors for Chapter 5 are the community partners. Their organizational affiliations follow:

Bart Epler is a fireman with the Bloomington (Indiana) Fire Department. At the time of the study described in Chapter 5, he was the program director for the city's Boys and Girls Club.

Joni Clark serves as the reverend of the Bethel African Methodist Episcopal Church in Bloomington, Indiana. Bethel is a predominately African American church that has served the community for more than 125 years.

William McCoy serves as founder and pastor of the Anointed Harvest Fellowship Church in Bloomington, Indiana. It is a multicultural, multiracial assembly.

The late **Gwen Paulk** was the director of African American Cultural Center at Indiana University in Bloomington. At the time of the study, she also served as the education director for Bethel African Methodist Episcopal Church.

Nancy Slough is Parent Involvement Coordinator for the Monroe County Head Start Program in Bloomington, Indiana. She has worked in social services for 23 years.

Chris Truelock is the director of the Banneker Westside Community Center in Bloomington, Indiana. He grew up in the Banneker neighborhood and graduated from Indiana University.